BREAKING
THE CYBER CODE

A Game Changer That Prepares Our Workforce and Secures the Future

Sakinah Tanzil

Breaking The Cyber Code
by
Sakinah Tanzil

Cover Design:	Cherrie Woods Publicist, Eclectic PR (info@eclecticpr.com)
Editing/Formatting:	Gloria Palmer Walker (movinonup57@yahoo.com)
Publisher:	STEM Coaching, LLC 29155 Northwestern Hwy STE 424 Southfield, MI 48034

Contact Information:

Coaching:	https://sakinahtanzilcoaching.as.me/
Company Website:	www.sakinahtanzil.com
Phone:	844-96-COACH
Facebook:	www.facebook.com/CoachSakinah
LinkedIn:	https://www.linkedin.com/in/sakinah-tanzil-000295187/
YouTube:	https://www.youtube.com/user/sakinahtanzil
ISBN:	978-1-7350271-0-4

ACKNOWLEDGEMENTS

American Association of University Women (AAUW)
CAPP Institute
Career One Stop
Cherrie Woods (Publicist)
CompTIA
Cybersecurity Ventures
Detroit Writing Room (Stephanie Steinberg)
Dr. Daniel Shoemaker (UDM)
Former U.S. President Barack Obama
GlassDoor.com
Gloria Palmer Walker (Editor)
IC3
Indeed.com
ISACA
ISC (2)
ITIL
National Initiative Cybersecurity Education (NICE)
National Institute of Standards and Technology (NIST)
NICE Workforce Management Working Group
PayScale.com
PositivePsychology.com
STEM.org
TheBalanceCareers.com
The Coaching Tools Company
Tony Stoltzfus
Two Sisters Publishing Writing Club (Elizabeth Ann Atkins)
United States Department of Commerce
V A Institute on Character (Ryan Niemiec)

DEDICATIONS

Thank you all for inspiring and motivating me to keep pursuing my dreams so this day could finally become a reality. For that very reason, this book is dedicated to you!

Zakiyyah Tanzil (Mother)

Abdullah Tanzil (Father)

Jameel Tanzil (Brother)

Akilah Ehioze (Daughter)

Akil Ehioze (Significant other)

Dr. Terrance Dillard (Professor/Mentor)

Dr. Daniel Shoemaker (Professor/Mentor)

City of Detroit, Michigan

Henry Ford College

Baker College

University of Detroit Mercy

Love,
Sakinah Tanzil

TABLE OF CONTENTS

Breaking The Cyber Code Series, Part Two

Foreword

Sakinah Tanzil's series, *Breaking the Cyber Code*, is a book that is long overdue. I served as a subject matter expert for both NICE 1.0 and the current 2.0 versions, and our intention with the Framework was to provide a logical set of workforce roles and knowledge/skill/ability (KSA) recommendations for practical use. However, the problem with monumental collections of best practices advice is they are hard for the average reader to digest and apply. That is why Sakinah's contribution is so valuable.

This is a personal experience piece with a very down-to-earth focus on how people who are not well-versed in the general practice of cybersecurity can find rewarding opportunities. The NICE Framework is authoritative, so it is an excellent point of reference for anybody who wants to get into the field. The actual job role classifications and the attendant KSAs can be confusing, and therefore, it is sometimes hard for an individual to visualize where they fit in. Sakinah's description of her own journey will let you fit your personal goals and life expectations into the path she has already broken for you.

More important, the Framework is full of lofty ideas that might not necessarily resonate with people who are not in the business of standard development and use. Sakinah's account looks at the profession from the perspective of an individual who is trying to make it in the field. Her unpretentious and practical narrative will give you a much better idea of how to focus your own energies and interests into a particular job role within a diverse work environment. In some respects, it is the affective elements of this discussion that carry the most significance since the field needs people and those people have to be able to visualize their place in the strange new world of threat and countermeasures.

Consequently, I highly recommend Sakinah's effort as a roadmap for people who have the desire to begin the journey but who might not know what direction to head. Sakinah provides clear guidance for people like that. This is a must-read for anybody interested in getting into the exciting new field of cybersecurity.

Dan Shoemaker, Ph.D.
Professor and Graduate Program Director
Center For Cyber Security And Intelligence Studies
University Of Detroit Mercy

Breaking the Cyber Code
Part 1

Introduction

I am Sakinah Tanzil, a life-long Detroiter who was educated in the Detroit Public School System. My first job was a paper route that I worked with my little sister at the age of twelve where I learned accountability, timeliness, and money management. My adult career was inspired by writing a paper about Bill Gates, the founder of Microsoft, and learning about the national Y2K problem with computers in the late 1990's. I was educated at Henry Ford College, where I obtained my Associate of Science in Computer Information Systems in 1999. I have worked as a flight attendant, entrepreneur, and real estate broker. I later obtained a Bachelor of Science in Information Technology and Security at Baker College in 2010.

My passion is learning new things and educational achievement, so I continued my educational track by obtaining a Master of Science in Information Assurance in 2012 and a Master of Science in Software Management in 2014 from the University of Detroit Mercy.

I worked on President Obama's working group to develop the Affordable Care Act, also known as Obamacare, which became national law. My cyber security career includes working at a cloud computing company and two health insurance plans, and I am presently working as an information security program manager at a nationally-recognized integrated healthcare system.

My Mission

As a certified cybersecurity career coach, my mission is to improve the lives of all, including underserved men, women, and children, by providing career, business, and life strategy tools so individuals can have sustainable and rewarding personal and professional lives in science, technology, engineering, and math (STEM) career fields.

My Purpose

I am in business to improve the lives of young professionals throughout the lifecycle of their careers. Whether you are just starting out in this career field or have had several years of experience in this industry, the opportunities are endless for you if you have the knowledge, skills, and abilities, and are eager to continuously learn.

My Goal

The goal of this book is to be your career guide and coach to help you better understand the opportunities out there so you can break into the cybersecurity industry where there are a tremendous amount of job opportunities and several hundred thousand vacancies on a daily basis that may be open to you right now.

Industry experts are projecting that by the year 2022, there will be at least three million job openings that will go unfilled in information technology positions due to a lack of qualified candidates. I am here to share with you information that I have to get you started in these lucrative, rewarding career fields.

National Initiative Cybersecurity Education (NICE) Assignments and Projects[1]

- I started working with the government on the NICE framework in Grad School in 2012.

- My work included mapping the very first knowledge, skills, abilities, and tasks that became the new framework.

- I currently participate on the NICE Working Group.

- I helped to author and write the published paper called *Cybersecurity Is Everyone's Job* in 2018.

---

[1] https://www.nist.gov/news-events/news/2018/10/ cybersecurity-everyones-job

BREAKING
THE CYBER CODE

Purpose

My purpose in this book is to provide information that is relevant to individuals who may be interested in a career in cybersecurity or other science, technology, engineering, and mathematics (STEM) fields, and need the resources and knowledge of where to start. When I first started out in the industry over twenty years ago, I could not find the mentors, advocates, sponsors, or coaches who could guide me and help me find the right tools and resources, so I want to be that advocate for you or any organization looking to build their cybersecurity teams.

My Narrative[2]

What does Sakinah's name mean?

I am spiritually intense and can sting or charm. My name brings love and new starts into life and attracts money. In business, I am the creator and promoter of original ideas and usually enjoy considerable financial success. I am bold, independent, inquisitive, and interested in research. I know what I want and why I want it.

I desire to inspire and lead, and to control others' affairs. I am giving, courageous, action-oriented, energetic, and

---

[2]   https://www.sevenreflections.com/name/sakinah/?switch=1

strong-willed. I want to make a difference in the world, and this attitude often attracts me to cultural interests, politics, social issues, and the cultivation of my creative talents.

BREAKING
THE CYBER CODE

My Background

Why do I support diversity and inclusion?

I am a living example of diversity and inclusion because my racial and ethnic background consists of Native American, African American, Asian American, and Caucasian American or European descent. When you see me, you know I am African American, but that is just one part of my DNA. As a result, I was subjected to much racism when I started my career in technology in the late 1990's.

I was the only black female in my classes at that time that I can remember, so I felt very ostracized. There was one other African American male in my classes, and we stuck together and helped each other along the way because we could relate to one another better and had similar life experiences. I don't remember a lot being mentioned about diversity and inclusion back then, but it was needed.

Today we hear about diversity and inclusion almost every day and so much progress has been made on this effort. There have been numerous reports done about the benefits of diversity and inclusion. Research studies have found that companies that support a diverse workforce have better financial performance, customer acquisition, market share, and employee and customer retention, and statistically do better than companies that are not diversified.[3]

---

[3]   https://www.mckinsey.com/business-functions/organization/our-insights/why-diversity-matters

Have You Experienced Unconscious Bias In Your Career?

Unconscious bias is a sneaky thing to deal with because it happens deep within our own psyche. It is built up over time based on our interactions with others and what we see and hear about in the media and in our surrounding communities. One thing for sure is we all have biases deep within us, sometimes unknowingly. It can be hard to change our subconscious minds if we do not know where the biases come from or have the skills or the know-how to correct them. Some examples of unconscious bias that have been circulating in the surrounding communities are, "All black people are lazy," or "All white people are racists," which have no factual bases, and furthermore, lump entire groups of people into one generic category, which does not leave room for individuality.

For that reason, we need to advocate for more diversity, inclusion, and equality in the workplace and even in our everyday personal encounters with people who may be different from us. Then we may be able to build healthier and stronger relationships with everyone. Furthermore, it will help us to better understand and communicate our differences to one another and change people's minds for the better. We can indeed co-exist and still have different lifestyles, cultures, religions, ethnic backgrounds, and personal family histories, and work together to create a vibrant world around us. When we do this, we will create a spectacular future for everyone involved and defeat this phenomenon called unconscious bias.

Gender Equality

How does the gender gap affect women's careers, families, and personal lives?

Across the world, women are struggling to make progress in politics, education, healthcare, leadership, income, and property rights or land ownership, to just name a few. And, here in the United States, we have made only incremental progress over the last one hundred years, when women first gained the right to vote. There still has not been nearly enough progress made in general in order to reach full gender equality.

Gender inequality affects women in their careers and in their everyday lives because women are not being considered for management roles, which then affects their salaries and future retirement plans. Recent studies in the United States have found that women are paid on average twenty percent less than a man working in the same roles, which in turn affects their entire families' quality of life. In addition, the statistics are dismal when it comes to the number of women executives leading Fortune 500 companies and working on company boards, even though women generally make most of the consumer buying decisions for their household.

At the current rate of progress, it could take at least anothe⁻ one hundred years to finally reach the goal of gender parity, and that is just unacceptable. There are several women's progressive organizations that are taking up these causes, and I am cautiously optimistic about the future. There is a real possibility that we could one day see a time in the future when men and women are considered equal human beings under the law in the home, in the workplace, and around the world. We must see more women being treated fairly in all these arenas of life because it is better for the world economy and future generations to come.

BREAKING
THE CYBER CODE

My Experience With Pay Equity And The Skills Needed To Ask For More

When I started out in the workforce, I had no idea what the going pay rate was for the job I was applying for and, therefore, accepted the pay offered because I just was excited to have the opportunity. Little did I know, I was being paid less than anyone else, including another man in the same role, because I did not ask for more or even know what to do to get more money. Through the years, as I changed jobs and even joined management roles, I still did not know I had the power to advocate for myself and request more money than the job opportunity offered by simply asking then negotiating my pay and being willing to walk away if need be.

When I started my first cybersecurity role after completing my master's degree, I knew I had the necessary education and experience to perform the role. For the first time, I researched online what the salary range was for that particular job title and went into the interview knowing what the starting rate was. At the interview, when I was being asked about my work experience, previous projects, and salary request, I made the big mistake of telling the interviewer the starting and ending salary ranges of the position, so he offered me the lowest pay rate and I did not counteroffer because I did not have the negotiation skills. I was too desperate to have the job, so I froze in the moment and immediately accepted the offer. This was a tremendous mistake on my part. I should have provided a counteroffer, negotiated my way up the income scale, and asked for as much as possible because I was in the driver's seat and that was my one opportunity to set my rate for that role before joining the team. This was devasting for my career because it set the income level for my roles moving forward and became the starting rate at the next job I decided to take just because that was what I had been paid at my previous employer.

According to the American Association of University Women (AAUW), which is the organization that has been working on these causes since 1881, pay equity and equal employment opportunity are matters of simple fairness. "The gender pay gap hurts women of all backgrounds, and it has far-reaching consequences for women's financial security. Women working full time in the United States typically are paid only eighty percent of what men are paid, and women of color are paid even less. The gender pay gap starts just one year out of college with women making eighty-two cents to a man's dollar, and the disadvantages only worsen over time. That's why it's crucial that women of all ages learn to negotiate a fair salary." (AAUW)

According to the AAUW Work Smart Online course, we need to prepare in advance of the interview and have a strategy in place before we even consider having this crucial conversation about pay with the employer. Below are some of their tips and tricks we should follow prior to the meeting:[4]

---

4   AAUW Work Smart Online Course and Workbook

Brainstorm ideas about your portfolio of experiences and write value statements of your accomplishments

a) Research the salaries for that role and know your target salary.

b) Research the company benefits package.

c) Know what your strategy will be going into the discussion.

d) Develop persuasive responses and role play with someone you trust.

e) Practice! Practice! Practice![5]

---

[5]   AAUW Quick Facts: https://www.aauw.org/what-we-do/ public-policy/aauw-issues/gender-pay-gap/

BREAKING
THE CYBER CODE

Are Your Career Health, Mental Health, And Physical Health Related?

Back in 2009, the president of the United States, Barack Obama, asked for citizens to volunteer to work to develop a new healthcare law which later became the Patient Protection and Affordable Care Act also known as the ACA, or in other circles as Obamacare. I signed up for that task and worked with his leadership team to ensure that certain preventive care benefits were included and even considered mandatory in the healthcare plan. We as participants wanted to be assured that pre-existing conditions also were a covered benefit and that preventive care such as men and women's health screenings for things such cancer, diabetes, depression, women prenatal care, and other mental health benefits was included. Even today, these very benefits are the most crucial coverages that people want to protect.

One of the benefits I personally fought for was healthcare coverage benefits for mentally ill patients. Mental illness had a negative and powerful stigma around it at the time and still does. Only now is it becoming safer to talk about it in our communities. Today, more and more people, such as celebrities, are opening up and becoming comfortable sharing their experiences with mental illness and other health issues, and this is helping so many families in a variety of ways. We really need to think about mental illness more as a brain disorder that affects on average one in five people in the U.S.

Mental health is all about the brain and it is a very important organ in our body that should be considered a part of our overall physical health. That is why exercise, meditation, eating healthier foods, getting the required amount of sleep, and enjoying fun activities with friends and family should be an integral part of a well-balanced life. Self-care and a healthy lifestyle create a positive life and well-being, which pays big dividends for your mind, your body, and your career.

The following are some cognitive behavioral therapy (CBT) tips and tricks courtesy of TherapistAid.com that I have learned could work wonders for you the next time you are having a stressful day. [6]

Distress Tolerance Skills (A.C.C.E.P.T.S.):

Activities: Engage in activities that require thought and concentration. This could be a hobby, project, work, or school.

Contributing: Focus on someone or something other than yourself. You can volunteer, do a good deed, or do anything else that will contribute to a cause or a person.

Comparisons: Look at your situation in comparison to something worse. Remember a time you were in more pain, or when someone else was going through something more difficult.

---

[6]   www.TherapistAid.com, Copyright 2005.

Emotions: Do something that will create a competing emotion. Feeling sad? Watch a funny movie. Feeling nervous? Listen to soothing music.

Pushing Away: Do away with negative thoughts by pushing them out of your mind. Imagine writing your problem on a piece of paper, crumbling it up, and throwing it away. Refuse to think about the situation until a better time.

Thoughts: When your emotions take over, try to focus on your thoughts. Count to ten, recite a poem in your head, or read a book.

Sensations: Find safe physical sensations to distract you from intense negative emotions. Wear a rubber band and snap it on your wrist, hold an ice cube in your hand, or eat something sour like a lime.

What Is Positive Psychology And How Can It Improve Your Life?

I am a Certified Personal Executive Coach and I received my coach training from The Coaching and Positive Psychology (CaPP) Institute. I learned many methodologies and frameworks during my certification training, but what motivated me the most was the science of Positive Psychology and how it helps to motivate and inspire us to reach our career, business, and life goals. Positive Psychology is the study of optimal living. This science answers the questions:[7]

a)   What makes people thrive?

b)   What fosters happiness? Resilience? Strengths?

c)   What is Positive Emotion?

d)   What are the good things about life?

Happiness is the only thing we pursue for its own sake. Everything else we pursue because we believe it will make us happier. Happiness is fifty percent genetic, forty percent our intentional choices, and ten percent our circumstances (CaPP Institute). Even though some people may be born with the genetic disposition for

---

[7]   Coaching and Positive Psychology Institute (CaPP) Training 2019

happiness, there are still ways we can become happier. In addition, we may not be able to change our circumstances when it comes to happiness, but we can become intentional about creating our own happiness. For that very reason, we can and should make intended choices that will boost our happiness quotient deliberately. Things such as having healthy relationships, having a purpose-driven career, being financially secure, and being ready for life's challenges are all planned actions we can control that will work wonders for our contentment and well-being.

We can and should do things that feel good to our mind, body, and spirit, like walking in nature, watching a feel-good show, reading a self-help book, participating in faith-filled activities, and any other specific actions that have brought us positive emotions, satisfaction, and meaning in the past. You do have a choice in improving your happiness, but you must be consistent and determined to do the work. Take every opportunity to live in the moment and be present in performing your everyday activities because in that very second is where the excitement lies.

Remember, let us be willing to focus on these things that bring us passion and pleasure in a healthy way by consciously taking positive steps that will create good emotions that will help us become even more resilient and content in our lives. If we do this, we will have the capacity and reserve to face our daily challenges head on, so we will not just be a conqueror, but we will thrive in any situation no matter what obstacles come our way.

BREAKING
THE CYBER CODE

What Is Resilience And How Can You Make It Work For You?

Resilience is the ability to bounce back from setbacks, and thrive, grow, and be effective in the face of adversity, challenges, and change. I have faced a lot of stressors and obstacles throughout my life, and as a result, those same experiences have strengthened me and made me more resilient and stronger than ever before. I would not have it any other way because it has given me a great deal of courage and has created a type of fearlessness that could have only occurred through challenges and radical change.

It now gives me some peace of mind to realize things could always be worse than they are and there are many people out there who may not have the same opportunities as I do, which makes me even more grateful to have the opportunities that come my way. You too can handle anything that comes your way by strength and perseverance.

Resilience is one concept of Positive Psychology, which is the research-based scientific body of knowledge related to happiness. It incorporates positive habits that have five building blocks of success:[8]

1.   Positive thinking: gratitude, optimism, self-awareness

2.   Social connection: kindness, relationships, community well-being

3.   Managing the negative: stress reduction, forgiveness, resilence

4.   Living in the moment: joy, savoring, flow

5.   Achievement: goals, meaning

Resilience can be taught and learned. It is largely about how you think, so you can make it work for you. Realizing that challenges will indeed come and knowing it is all about how you deal with those challenges could be the determining factors of your success. Just remember: We all experience bad days, but we must not be defeated. We must get back up and try again. Therefore, to sustain happiness and maintain resilience, we must face adversity head on with a plan of action and a resolve that we are all more than fighters—we are overcomers.

---

8   Coaching & Positive Psychology (CaPP) Institute Training 2019.

BREAKING
THE CYBER CODE

What Will You Do With Your 168 Hours In A Week To Get The Things You Want To Do Done?

Time management is a very important concept to encourage in one's life because we all have things we would like to get done if only we had enough time in our day to do them. I had to learn fast in school and work about making proper use of my time. In school, there was studying, homework assignments, research papers due, presentational speeches, and a whole lot of deadlines. It required me to stay on top of my duties on a regular basis or I possibly would have flunked out of my educational program.

At a previous employer, I had to learn time management immediately because my boss documented every minute I was at work and fired many workers because they could not get to work on time. We all have 24 hours in a day/168 hours in a week/365 days in a year to get things done. We must try to use that time wisely and productively or we will not meet our personal and professional obligations.

When you want to better understand how to use your time, try taking a week to document and track what you do each hour and what you spend the most time on each day. Start with the things you do first thing in the morning and make note of everything you do throughout the day. Keep a daily journal of each task required of you and how long it takes to get it all done. Your goal is to track your daily activities for an entire week to get an understanding of what you spend your time on.

Once 7 days have been tracked, go back to your activity journal and review how much you got done and the required time it took. Pay special attention to what tasks took up much of your time and determine what time of day would be most productive for you to get the critical tasks done. Identify where your time wasters are, such as, surfing the internet, watching television, or spending a lot of time on your phone. Determine what are the most significant tasks that need to be done that can only be done by you. Then determine which tasks can be delegated to others, if possible.

Start to plan out a new weekly calendar with this detailed information of the tasks and the time it takes from your tracking exercise. I recommend you use an electronic calendar or other scheduler and set time reminders for each task in allocated time slots that work best for you. Once you have an ideal week planned out and have scheduled the time to do them, try to implement those tasks as soon as you can. Remember, some tasks will pop up that are out of your control, so be flexible and nimble and adjust your calendar when necessary.

We tend to think some items will take longer than expected, but you will be surprised that once you have scheduled a designated time for a task and you spend very deliberately-focused time on completing that task, you will be able to free up more time to add or remove unnecessary activities. Here comes the fun part: now you can add in some new exciting activities that will bring you joy, peace, and serenity. This is how you find balance in the days and weeks ahead.

BREAKING
THE CYBER CODE

S.M.A.R.T.E.R. Goal Planning

Accord ng to Google.com, the first known use of the term S.M.A.R.T. occurs in the November 1981 issue of *Management Review* by George T. Doran. In recent history, the letters "E" and "R" were added for the purposes of continuous improvement in the goal-setting achievement lifecycle. Below are the S.M.A.R.T.E.R. acronym definitions:[9]

Specific: A specific goal should clearly state what you want to accomplish, why it is an important goal, and how you intend to accomplish the goal.

Measurable: A measurable goal should include a plan with targets and milestones you can use to make sure you're moving in the right direction.

Attainable: An attainable goal should be realistic and include a plan that breaks your overall goal down into smaller, manageable action steps that use the time and resources available to you within the timeline you've set.

---

[9]   How to Set and Accomplish Goals
       https://www.pinterest.com/pin/451908143859982406/

Relevant: A relevant goal should be realistic when measured against your business model, mission statement, market, client base, and industry.

Time-Based: A time-based goal is limited by a defined period and includes a specific timeline for each step of the process.

Evaluative: A continuous way to evaluate the progress being made so you identify how things are going on the journey of obtaining your goal.

Revisable: A revisable goal is a way to adjust for the unexpected, and update or re-align the goal so it suits the changeable situation while still being able to meet the desired goal.

Bad Example: I want to lose weight by exercising and eating healthier.

Better Example: I want to lose 100 pounds within 1 year by exercising 5 days a week for at least 45 minutes and maintain a 1400-calorie diet of healthier meals by tracking my food and dairy intake daily. If I get off track on any day, I will immediately re-adjust for the next day and get back on track with my original set goals.

Make sure to write your goals down on paper and keep them somewhere you can see them. Create an action plan with step-by-step activities of how you will meet the goal with deadlines attached to them. Have a system to track and automate your process, and adjust and re-adjust when needed. Remember to evaluate your progress along the way on a regular basis and be flexible with your methods but not with your goal. Do not be too hard on yourself when experiencing a setback and try to enjoy the journey along the way. Think of healthy and exciting ways to celebrate small wins and reward yourself for making progress.

What Is Productivity And How Can It Improve The Way I Get Things Done?

Are you wondering why successful people seem to always be living their best life, managing to spend time with family and friends while running a lucrative business or having a sustainable, fulfilling career? These people are always taking those lavish vacations, and they have the big, beautiful home, new luxury cars, and seem to have it all figured out.

The fact is we all have the capacity to get more done in less time and live that life if we just become more deliberate and intentional with the way we use our time. What it takes is some focus and some upfront planning on a daily, weekly, monthly, and quarterly basis that sets us up for a profitable year. If it is good for Fortune 500 corporations, it is good for us too. We do this by figuring out how to get things done more effectively and efficiently with the 24 hours we already have in the most fruitful way possible.

The term is called productivity and we all can do more with less if we are more specific in what type of actions we take and work in the present moment. *"Productivity is defined as the efficient use of resources, labor, capital, land, materials, energy, information, in the production of various goods and services. Higher productivity means accomplishing more with the same amount of resources or achieving higher output in terms of volume and quality from the same input."* All of us are given the same amount of capacity relatively speaking; it is just that we use our time in different ways on things we believe are the most important. If we take the time to plan on the things that matter, we can get more valuable use of our precious resources and positive energy.

One way I try to get more done and stay on track with my goals is to set aside some time every week for planning on the things I want to accomplish for the upcoming week. I also think through what it will take to achieve those goals on a more granular level by identifying what steps I will need to take and documenting them. Then I put those specific tasks in my electronic calendar, so I do not forget what I need to do, then I work that plan.

Another helpful tip is to pretend you will have to write a weekly status report and send it to your boss and yourself so he or she knows what progress you are making on those goals. This will help you to stay on top of your progress. Track your work daily by using automation tools so it is easier to report on at the end of each week. I try to plan out my goals for at least 3 months in advance, based on my original annual objectives, and adjust the plan when needed, as things will come up along the way.

As you make progress, try to measure the percentage of completion in concrete terms and reward yourself on any advancements you have made along the way. Soon, you will be on your way to massive results if you do the work required.[10] [11]

---

[10]   Ministry of Employment, Immigration and Civil Status Republic of Seychelles: http://www.employment.gov.sc/ what-is-productivity.

[11]   Brian Moran and Michael Lennington (2013), The 12 Week Year: Get More Done in 12 Weeks Than Others Do In 12 Months, John Wiley & Sons, Inc.

BREAKING
THE CYBER CODE

What Are You Doing To Develop Yourself Personally And Professionally?

If we want to get ahead and reach our full potential, taking the time to work on self-improvement and investing in new skills or obtaining new knowledge is essential to our success in life personally and professionally. The *Business Dictionary*[12] defines personal development as the process of improving oneself through such activities as enhancing employment skills, increasing consciousness, and building wealth.

I thrive on being able to learn new things that will benefit my well-being and career options because this world is full of fascinating wonders that can inspire us and teach us to be better at all almost everything. I remember when I first started my career in the tech industry. I was mesmerized by all the possibilities and the future opportunities to improve my life and the world. I recommend that everyone try to immerse themselves in something new every single year by creating a self-development plan to improve their future chances of success. If you want career advancement, then professional development is key to moving on up.

---

[12] http://www.businessdictionary.com/definition/personal-development.html

"Professional development consists of learning activities that improve knowledge and skills related to your career. It can range from a one-hour webinar to a four-year college degree." (Career One Stop)[13]

Finding ways to improve your employability by participating in career enhancement activities such as courses, workshops, lectures, coaching, and even going back to school for higher education will more than likely improve your odds of getting that company raise or landing that new business opportunity. It could be as simple as reading a self-help book that will boost one of your strengths, improving on a personal weakness, or providing a missing skill your organization needs to fulfill its mission. Remember, it is never too late and you are never too old to learn something new because the world is massive and overflowing with exciting things to do and learn that are waiting to be discovered, and as a result, life keeps teaching us every single day.

---

[13]   https://www.careeronestop.org/ExploreCareers/Plan/ professional-development.aspx

BREAKING
THE CYBER CODE

What Is Coaching And How Could It Enhance Your Life?

Coaching is partnering with clients in a thought-provoking and creative process that inspires them to maximize their personal and professional potential. A professional coaching relationship exists when coaching includes a business agreement or contract that defines the responsibilities of each party. (ICF[14]) Coaching has been a tremendous benefit for me personally in my business, career, and life. That is why I feel strongly about coaching and started my own coaching business. Coaching helps millions of people around the world every year in achieving their goals.

I obtained my first career coach in 2016 and it was my introduction to this type of expertise. I was in a new position and the organization I was working for offered coaching services as an employee benefit. I signed up for the services and met with the coach, not knowing what to expect. To my surprise, she had a coaching framework where she wanted to help me understand myself better and wanted to determine my personality traits and work style to see how I showed up for myself in my current role. It was very interesting because I had never had a personalized assessment up to this point in my career such as this one that tested my temperament and

---

14   Internctional Coach Federation https://coachfederation.org/

management style. The experience was intriguing, but at the same time, I had no agenda, so I brought no real action items to the engagement. We only worked on what the coach thought was needed at the time. After the encounter, I wanted more, but this time I wanted to have a plan and work on things that would help me advance in my role. So, I sought out a new coach to help me in the areas that would strengthen my leadership skills and improve on my strengths and weaknesses. To do that, I had to make a bigger investment of my own money for my personal development and find someone who had demonstrated success in those areas I wanted to improve myself in at the time. I set aside money in my budget that would be specifically allocated for annual personal and professional development on a continuous basis, and the rest is history. Every year moving forward, I have been investing in myself with my own money for professional development and it has helped me develop into the person I am today. I recommend that you devote time and money in your future growth that will help you advance your goals because it is so worth it.

BREAKING
THE CYBER CODE

Why Is Finding A Mentor So Crucial To Your Career Development?[15]

Finding a mentor is so crucial to your career development because you will need someone who has gone before you and done the work you want to do on your career journey. When I first started out in my career field in the late 1990's, I had no mentors and it was detrimental to my career. I had a very hard time landing a job and had no one to guide me and motivate me to keep going. As I look back on those days, I wonder how my life would have been different if I had had a mentor.

Anyone has the capability to be a mentor to someone else because you do not have to be an expert to want to help people. You just need to want to do it and believe in the person you are mentoring. I have made mentoring one of my top priorities because I do not want anyone else to feel lost like I did when no one was available to help me. You will want to limit how many people you mentor at the same time because you will not have a lot of time to mentor everyone, so make sure the person(s) you

---

15   Maxwell, John C. (2010) The Complete 101 Collection: What Every Leader Needs to Know, Nashville Tennessee, Thomas Nelson Inc.

are mentoring is open and flexible around your schedule and is willing to do the necessary work that is required.

You will need to show and tell your mentee how to do things, so be prepared to invest a lot of time and energy into your mentee. Give them a lot of opportunities to watch you in action and give the mentee opportunities to demonstrate based on your instruction and to re-enact some of the teachings. Your mentorship engagement period could possibly take months, or maybe even years, because you want to get the mentee to a point where they can do things on their own without your guidance. You may have to provide tools and resources to fuel the mentee in his or her efforts to achieve their career goals. That is why mentoring is a serious investment and not everyone has the resources to do this kind of work.

As a mentor, the goal should be to build others up so you have a successor in the industry who will in turn invest in more people by mentoring the next generation. The joy you will have seeing your mentee succeed in their career goals will be exhilarating and motivational, and as a result, you will be making the world around you a better tomorrow.

How Using Your Knowledge To Consult Others Can Benefit Your Career And Build Work History

If you have previous work experiences and a history of successes in a certain industry or job function and have developed needed skills that are in high demand, you have the capability to consult others in those specific areas and build even more work experiences. You will need to be very proficient, knowledgeable, and professional, and be able to communicate effectively in order to make a difference in the consulting business.

Consulting is the act of counseling and advising others in a specific discipline or subject matter that you have mastered or have had accomplishments in helping others and have achieved some level of expertise and wins for yourself and others.

For IT consultants, technical competence is essential, but it is not enough. If you want to be a sought-after resource as a technician and become a consultant, you must master communication, collaboration, and human relationship skills. In short, you must become a skilled and trusted advisor. (Freedman, 2000[16])

The consulting process consist of five steps:

1. Understand the current state.

2. Define the desired state.

3. Analyze the gap between these states.

4. Recommend an action plan to move from the current state to the desired state.

5. Partner with the client to implement the action plan.

I have had a lot of interesting jobs in the past that have helped me be a better employee, contractor, manager, collaborator, team member, and leader for other companies even when I thought I was not going to benefit from those job roles. I have worked as a retail sales assistant manager, real estate agent and broker, and a restaurant owner, and I believe all of those job functions have developed me into the person and valued team player I am today. So, do not be afraid to take those seemingly-meaningless jobs that are unique and challenging because you never know how those skills can transfer and help you with your new consulting roles and other future ventures.

---

[16]   Freedman, Rick (2000): IT Consultant, A Commonsense Framework for Managing the Client Relationship, Jossey-Bass/Pfeiffer, San Francisco, CA

What Is The Difference Between A Counselor And A Coach?

Counselors are healthcare professionals who help people with mental health issues that affect everyday life. I am a true believer in mental well-being, and getting a counselor can help you have a healthier mindset and build self-esteem. There are so many known benefits to obtaining this kind of care, but there are distinctions between receiving services from a counselor and receiving services from a coach. Below are some of the remedies and healthcare outcomes that a counseling service provider can help a patient alleviate.[17]

Counseling services can:

- Help you alleviate anxiety.

- Help you improve self-confidence.

- Help you improve relationships.

- Help you with emotional balance.

- Help you increase assertiveness skills.

- Help you handle stress better.

---

[17] Benefits of Counseling, Professional Development Image, www.pinterest.com

- Help you set stronger boundaries.

- Help you deal with trauma resolution.

Coaching, on the other hand, sometimes feels like counseling, but it is not. Some coaching certification programs teach psychology science and coaches do provide a confidential, safe space for you to solve your own dilemmas, but it is not at all a substitute for mental health services. As a coach, we will try our best to help you achieve your personal and professional life goals; however, we are not licensed to provide mental health counseling and should not try to do so. If we do believe you are better served by getting additional mental healthcare treatment, we will direct you to those additional resources so you can indeed get all the required help you need in order to move forward in your life.

How Can I Find Internships So I Can Get The Job Experience I Need?[18]

It is never too early to start thinking about how you are going to get work experience in your chosen career field or industry. You do not want to wait until the very last minute either because you will run the risks of being left behind with no career options and being desperate, frustrated, and very discouraged because you were not proactive in finding the right opportunity in advance.

Internships are a great way to receive real-world, hands-on experience so you can find out what job roles and functions you like and dislike, and what types of business areas interest you the most. When I first attended college, I knew what field I wanted to study in and picked my degree program, but my career path was very new and most job functions had not been developed yet. The first year I attended college, I wanted to stay focused on my studies and did not think of the jobs I wanted ahead of time, but it stayed in the back of my mind as I progressed in my program. It wasn't until I was three months from graduating with my degree that I realized I needed to

---

[18] How to Get an Internship: A Guide for College Students, https://www.glassdoor.com/blog/guide/how-to-get-an-internship/

determine what to do next to get some work experience. That was a big mistake.

I believe the more you have an idea of what you want to do before you pursue your degree program and have an idea of what the end game will be like, the better prepared you can be when the time comes. At the time of graduation, I went to the college career resource center to ask for help and to see if they knew what jobs were available to me. I worked with a career advisor and they coached me on things like how to dress and how to conduct myself on a job interview. We researched local businesses in the area to see where my new skills and degree would be of good use.

I believe I met with the advisor on a weekly basis to learn as much as possible to try to be ready for that new job opportunity. I was determined and open to doing anything necessary to get a job. The error I believe I made was that I had no idea or vision of the type of role I wanted, and I had not done the earlier work to identify what companies I wanted to work for when I graduated. I also did not know of anyone who had been on this path before, such as mentors, coaches, or sponsors, who could show me the right things to do for success. I had no idea of what to expect and did not have the best chance of landing a job because I had not properly prepared.

Do not make the same mistake I did of waiting until you are finished with your degree to start looking for a job. As soon as you have made up your mind what area of study you want to pursue, immediately start preparing a list of companies you want to work for and what job roles match your skill set. Start reaching out to people in your network you can talk to and find out what the work culture is like and what jobs are currently available in those companies.

According to Glassdoor.com, there are several strategies and tips you should consider when you are trying to find the right internship so you can have the best chance of landing that new role.

a. Consider your past experiences and see how they align with the positions out there.

b. Think about your degree program and see what knowledge, skills, and abilities you already have for the position for which you are applying.

c. Identify the transferrable skills you bring that will help you in those positions of choice.

d. Know what interests you have and try to find those roles that would be a match for those known interests.

e. Know where to look for jobs:

    • Jobsites

    • College career resources

    • Leverage your network

    • Contact companies directly

f. Build your resumé with these key factors in mind:

    • Use the S.T.A.R. method (situation, task, action, result) to explain past work history.

    • Try to quantify how you improved on the organization's bottom line.

    • Mention any awards or accomplishments you have.

    • Identify the skills, responsibilities, and key wins you have had in the past.

g. Ensure that your social media profiles are professional.

If you consider all these tools and act on them early on in your job search, you will be better off in the long run and will have the best odds of landing that internship or new role which is the best fit for you.

How Volunteering Can Land You The Job You Never Could Have Dreamed

There was a long period after my first college degree back in 1999 that I could not find work in my chosen field, and believe me, I tried everything I could think of at the time. The tech industry was very new, and I think no one knew what to do with someone like me, a new college graduate, minority woman with little industry experience. There were no career mentors, coaches, or sponsors I could get advice from, so I was very frustrated and lost. For that reason, I decided to put a pause on my search to find a job in my chosen field because the opportunities just were not available.

Fast forward almost 10 years after the tech industry boom, with many tech businesses created, more colleges with computer degrees, new IT certification programs, and a proven track record as a lucrative industry to have a career. There were finally many more openings for people who had the knowledge and skills to get the job done. By this time, I had had several different industry experiences, unrelated to IT, that I had done, but those jobs were influenced by technology because every business needed computers to improve their business practices. Even though I did not hold a specific IT role, I volunteered to implement computers for the many organizations I worked for and even did free work at other organizations that needed a new computer system. I did not have all the skills at the time, but with the help of the internet, I researched discussion boards, blogs, books, signed up for certification classes, and did a lot of homework on my own time and learned on the job too.

I am telling you this to let you know, if you cannot find the job you want, you can still set up a computer lab at home, volunteer at local businesses or nonprofits, buy computer books, join computer associations, and see what initiatives you can be a part of to get the skills you need to land the job you want. I was determined, and I was not going to give up and let my education go to waste because I knew deep down I was meant to do this kind of work.

What I am saying to you is you do not have to give up on this career field, even if you do not see a way to create the job you desire. The job I have today was obtained by volunteering at a newly-founded association where I maintained their communications system and helped the employer groups there with any issues they had. I impressed them so much that one of the organizations hired me to work directly for them. So, you see you never know where that new opportunity will come from. You just need to be open and willing to learn and take on the interesting assignments, paid or unpaid, so you can get those lovely recommendation letters that you can gather and save to share with potential employers. They will help you stand out from the rest of the applicants because you took the initiative and showed the drive and commitment to gain the skills necessary for the future.

As a result, I now have my dream job because I did not give up on myself, even when the going got tough. I studied and continued to keep up my IT skills and experience, so when the opportunity came, I was ready.

How Finding A Sponsor Can Help You In Your Career

If you are just starting out in your career, or even if you are a career veteran in your industry, your prospects and advancement opportunities will be so much more plentiful if you have someone on the inside advocating for you. This person is not a mentor who shares their guidance and advice, or a family member who has limited knowledge on your specific business area when needed. No; this person I am speaking of is what you call a sponsor.

What is a sponsor, you ask? According to TheLadders.com,[19] "A sponsor goes to bat on your behalf. The sponsor already works at the company where you want to work or want to get promoted."

Finding and securing a sponsor in the company you work for or the company you want to work for is not easy and it takes some intentional work. This person should be in a senior role and have some decision-making power so he or she can make a difference. You need to try to seek this person out and build a strong relationship with them by showing them that you are committed, trustworthy, and

---

[19]   https://www.theladders.com/career-advice/heres-what-a-career-sponsor-is-and-why-you-might-want-one

reliable. Try to find opportunities to prove to this person that you have what it takes to advance the vision, mission, and organizational goals which will benefit everyone.

The sponsor may have a different leadership style or role, and you may or may not share the same background or history with them, but this person has power and connections and can move the needle for you on new company projects, new roles, and promotions if they believe in you. Make every effort to have quality time with this person and do not be afraid to share your skills, education, training, and future career goals that you believe will help the sponsor better understand what you want and bring to the table.

Sponsors want to help the right kind of people succeed because it helps them in their career advancement and improves the organization's bottom line. Look for those visible opportunities which will make a positive impact and show them you have what it takes to make a difference. Remember to always do your best and continue to deliver quality work and meet company deadlines, which will help you become a strong leader and team player. Put in the necessary work effort and show the sponsor that you are ready to take the lead and do bigger things if given the chance to do so. I found my sponsor on my team, and when the right opportunity came along, I had a strong advocate in the room speaking on my behalf. I was able to land the opportunity I could have only dreamed of that allowed me to do some exciting things and lead the entire team, all because I proved to him I was capable and willing to do my best work every time.

How Apprenticeships Can Help You Get The On-the-Job Training You Need To Start That Career

According to Careeronestop.org, "Apprenticeships provide affordable pathways to high-paying jobs and careers without the typical student debt associated with college. And, more than 90 percent of apprentices remain employed after completing their program, and their average starting wage is more than $60,000. Over their careers, apprentices earn $300,000 more than workers who did not complete an apprenticeship." (Career One Stop, 2019[20])

Lately, people have been trying to avoid the cost of college and getting into student loan debt and therefore apprenticeships could be another option for getting that career you want by way of job training and hands-on experience without the high cost. What is even more rewarding is that you get paid while you learn and earn and gain that industry knowledge and work history at the same time, so it has wonderful advantages. Businesses are starting to develop these career pathway opportunities because they are having a very difficult time finding the right candidates with the skills needed to

---

[20] https://www.careeronestop.org/FindTraining/Types/
apprenticeships.aspx

expand their businesses and meet their organizational goals. That is why apprenticeships can be a possible solution for filling these specialized roles.

I believe this type of option would be a win-win situation for the employer and the employee because everyone would benefit from the experience. I am now more and more becoming an advocate for apprenticeship programs, and I think more companies should consider this benefit to fill the skills gap that currently exist. There are new resources becoming available every day and businesses are developing new programs. So, seek these opportunities out, and if you find that an organization does not have program, ask them if they are interested in starting one. You can find a current list of available apprenticeship programs at www. Apprenticeship.gov, and you can also research new ways and ideas on how to create one at your organization.

BREAKING
THE CYBER CODE

Professional Industry Associations Can Be Great Places To Find Jobs And Network With Individuals And Employers

I remember when I first started out in the technology industry, there weren't many resources or support groups where you could meet and network with other people in similar professions such as are available today. The tech industry was very new in the late 1990's and a lot of people were not aware of all the job opportunities and training resources available to them. Now, there are numerous organizations and professional industry associations that offer many resources, such as education, training, scholarships, and other support systems, that create ways to connect with like-minded individuals and employers with employment opportunities. There are all kinds of interesting professional associations for almost any specific group you can think of and that is a wonderful thing to witness today. I recently read that there are at least 35 industry associations and initiatives for women and minority groups available around the country.

I have heard of some good and some not-so-good experiences with some of the lesser-known professional associations. Make sure you come to the group with a specific mission and goal in mind so you can make the most of the time and networking opportunities with the right people. Some of these industry associations have membership fees or dues, so make sure you find out what those costs are so you can gain access to their resources. There also may be industry certifications the association offers. Research those resources also to find out what skills and training are more relevant to the job you are aiming for and if there are any additional requirements necessary for the obtainment of the certification or credential.

Below I have provided a list of well-known information technology and privacy associations that may provide the training and other resources you are looking for to build your IT career.

Professional Industry Associations:

1. ASIS International

2. Association of Computing Machinery (ACM)

3. Association of Information Technology Professionals (AITP)

4. Association of Software Professionals (ASP)

5. Computing Technology Industry Association (CompTIA)

6. IEEE Computer Society

7. Information Systems Security Association (ISSA)

8. International Association of Privacy Professionals (IAPP)

9. International Information System Security Certification Consortium (ISC^2)

10. Information System Audit and Control Association (ISACA)

What Hard And Soft Skills Do You Have That Will Help In Your Career Goals

Employers have many lofty demands and sometimes they want a super-human who must meet every single skill set and job requirement or else the applicant will be considered not qualified for the position needing to be filled. I am here to tell you that it is sometimes impossible to meet every requirement being requested because the person writing the job description may or may not understand the position being considered or the level of skill needed to accomplish the job being requested. That is why it is best to understand your own talents, skills, and abilities so you can demonstrate to the recruiter that you have the experience and expertise for the role during the interview process.

There are some skills all employers will be looking for when trying to find the best candidate, which are sometimes called hard and soft skill sets. Employers ultimately want a job applicant to have a hybrid of both types of skills for them to succeed in the new role. Below is a list of some of the types of hard and soft skills employers want when looking for the best candidate to do the job.[21]

Hard Skills

- Proficiency in a foreign language
- College degree or certificate
- Machine operation expertise
- Computer programming

Soft Skills

- Communication
- Motivation
- Flexibility
- Persuasion
- Leadership
- Work ethic
- Teamwork
- Positive attitude
- Time management
- Patience
- Problem-solving abilities

Hard skills can be taught in school or in on-the-job training, so employers are not so much fixated on whether you have an overwhelming knowledge of these skills because they can be learned. Soft skills, on the other hand, are the most sought-after skills by employers because they are interpersonal skills which are harder to master if you do not already possess them. So, when

---

[21]   https://www.thebalancecareers.com/hard-skills-vs-soft-skills-2063780

interviewing for any new role, be sure to try to display these suggested hard and desired soft skills by giving real-world examples of how you demonstrated these qualities in a previous environment, and you may increase your chances of landing the job and possibly having a bright career.

BREAKING
THE CYBER CODE

What Is Imposter Syndrome And How We Can Overcome This Feeling

Have you ever had that weird feeling someone was going to find out you do not deserve to be in the position you are in or that you are not really capable of getting that new leadership role with the higher salary and great perks, even though you have worked very hard to get to this day? You meet all the qualifications and experience, but still something in the back of your brain is telling you that you are not ready to lead. You think you don't deserve to go after your dream job because you feel you are not good enough to level up to the new challenges that may come.

Well, you are not alone. Many people at one time or another feel they do not have the knowledge, skills, or abilities to go after their life goals, and that somehow and someway, others are going to find out and it will not turn out well for them. I am here to tell you that I have felt that feeling numerous times throughout my entire career, and it still happens to me every time I want to go after a new project or when I decide to stretch myself in a challenging new way that I may have not experienced before.

According to ImposterSyndrome.com[22], "The only way to stop feeling like an impostor is to stop thinking like an impostor." (2019). Imposter syndrome is a very tricky thing that our brain does, and in a strange way, it is trying to protect us from things it thinks may harm us. The mind wants us to stay in our comfort zone where we can be safe and secure. Our brain struggles with a lot of change because change can be hard. We must combat this feeling of fear with new facts and realistic scenarios along with positive re-enforcement so that something good can be expected from the new experience.

Here are four tips we can practice to help combat imposter syndrome and move us forward with achieving our goals:

1.   Separate feelings from fact. Try to journal your negative thoughts and replace them with positive experiences from your past where you did succeed, or maybe the situation did not turn out as bad as you first thought.

2.   Recognize when you should feel fraudulent. If the challenge is new to you and you have never had this kind of experience before, realizing it is only normal to feel this way can help.

3.   Develop a new response to failure and mistake making. We all make mistakes and that is how we learn new ways of doing things better in the future, so embrace the newness of it all.

4.   Try to avoid expecting the worst will happen and instead replace those thoughts with a new positive

---

[22]   Imposter Syndrome: https://impostorsyndrome.com/10-steps-overcome-impostor/

script because, let's face it, we cannot predict the future.

Remember life is full of possibilities, and if we do not take advantage of the opportunities that come our way, we will never know what new exciting things await us in this very precious life we have here on earth. Therefore, be bold and courageous and do not fear; the future will be bright.

BREAKING
THE CYBER CODE

Know What Your Core Workplace Values Are And How They Can Help You Determine If An Organization Is A Good Fit For You

When I first started out on my career journey, I had no idea if any of the organizations or companies I was applying for was a good fit for me or my values. I did not have the luxury of determining it at the time, or even know what I expected from a workplace environment. I just had a goal of being gainfully-employed and needed to get a job so I could start making money right away. I say that to say some people may still be in that situation today and may not have the comfort of choosing the best fit for them because it may not be their current priority. Hopefully, that will become an option for you sooner than later, so you get off to a great start. I did remember researching the companies and reading their mission and vision statements, but that was the best-case scenario of what I knew to do to determine if I wanted to work for that company.

Today, people more and more are holding organizations accountable for their actions and want them to have purpose, mission, vision, and value statements that reflect a wide variety of traits, such as honesty, integrity, justice, fairness, and equal opportunity for all, just to name a few.

According to CareerOneStop.org[23], "Values are your beliefs about what is important or desirable. When your values line up with how you live and work, you tend to feel more satisfied and confident. Living or working in ways that contradict your values can lead to dissatisfaction, confusion, and discouragement. So, there is good reason to clarify your values and seek to match your work to them."

Now that I have more insight into what I want from an organization and know what I value based on my previous experiences, I try to work in an environment or job where I can thrive, and I am more deliberate about which companies I choose to work for. I also want to make sure, if I work for an organization or patronize a business, I want to trust that this company is being a good corporate citizen. Thankfully, it is becoming more possible for you to be in a situation to identify what your work values are and choose optimal positions which align with your beliefs and value system.

According to Indeed.com[24], below is a list of core workplace values to consider when determining which company aligns with your most-important workplace values:

---

[23]　https://www.indeed.com/career-advice/career-development/core-values

[24]　https://www.careeronestop.org/ExploreCareers/Assessments/work-values.aspx

- Acceptance
- Achievement
- Adventure
- Bravery
- Community
- Creativity
- Curiosity
- Family
- Friendship
- Growth
- Happiness
- Hard Work
- Honesty
- Humility
- Ingenuity
- Innovation
- Integrity
- Kindness
- Knowledge

- Open Communication
- Optimism
- Patience
- Peace
- Popularity
- Power
- Quality
- Respect
- Responsibility
- Spirituality
- Stability
- Success
- Tenacity
- Time Management
- Wealth
- Wisdom
- Work/Life Balance

There are work value assessments available to you so you can better understand what situations and environments are most favorable to you based on how you respond to the questions. Ask around about certain organizations and cultures, and be mindful of whether a company has a very toxic, competitive work environment. Remember, you have choices, and you do not have to settle for anything.

BREAKING
THE CYBER CODE

Know What Strengths You Have Already Inside You

When I was in kindergarten, my teacher noticed there was something different about me versus the other students and called my parents to the school to have a meeting about me. I was not part of the meeting and probably would have not understood what was happening, but on the way home from school that day, while walking with my father, he told me about the conversation. He said the teacher thought I was extremely advanced in my knowledge and abilities. She recommended I skip the first grade and go straight to second grade because I would be at a more appropriate level with my peers.

When my father told me about it, I was very excited and happy about the possibility, but my father stubbornly said to me right away that he did not want me to skip any grade levels. He wanted me to get more social skills and not miss out on any of my childhood development by advancing me too fast. I was devastated at the time because I thought it would be a great opportunity for me to finish school sooner so I could go to college as early as possible and help my struggling family someday. My dad had the final word, so it was settled. I did not get double promoted that day and maybe I am better off for it; I will never know.

Looking back, I would say I have always been smart and inquisitive and asked a lot of intriguing questions to get to the bottom of things. That has been a strength of mine for as long as I can remember. We all have strengths that makes us stand out and we should never be afraid to build on those strengths or any other superpowers to help us excel in our personal and professional lives. I was not able to benefit from my talents back then, but as I grew older, those strengths have gotten me into places I would have not thought possible.

According to the VIA Character Survey[25], I have the strength called "love of learning" that keeps me continuously reading, researching, and discovering new information at every chance I can get, which has benefited me my whole life. You also have strengths that are unique and helpful, and it is up to you to discover what those are and use them to improve your environment. Take the VIA character survey today, discover what your top strengths are, and build on them every day.

---

[25]   www.viacharacter.org

Virtue Of Temperance: Strength Of Prudence, Caution, Or Discretion

According to the Merriam-Webster Dictionary[26], temperance is defined as moderation in action, thought, feeling, or having restraint for something.

As a young teenager in high school, I did very little thinking before acting or being cautious—or better yet, using restraint in every situation. I wanted to be with the cool kids and have fun when away from home because that was all the freedom I had at the time. My family had a lot of serious everyday struggles to deal with, which were sometimes very depressing and exhausting due to the many financial problems we encountered and all the moving from place to place because we had a big family which required bigger housing. My mother needed to provide for us as a single parent on her own after she separated from my father. Nowadays, when I look back at the difficult decisions my mother had to make, I realize she did what was best for me and my siblings, and I am so grateful to her to this very day.

The Values in Action (VIA) Institute recognizes twenty-four unique character strengths we all have to some

---

[26]   https://www.merriam-webster.com/dictionary/temperance

degree, and prudence is one of them. "Prudence is associated with productivity and the ability to be conscientious, mostly likely because the prudent person tends not to enter into agreements unless he or she believes there is a good chance of a successful outcome." (Niemiec and McGrath, 2019[27])

There will be many instances where you may want to use your discretion and there are many instances where you will need to act fast in a situation or you may miss out on a fantastic opportunity. You will need to be mindful of the different circumstances and try not to overuse or underuse the act of being prudent. In fact, there is a fine balance between using your discretion and being productive, so in certain situations, you may have to use your intuition to guide you in making that best decision. In those cases, use your brain and your heart to take the necessary steps you believe are best for you with all the information you have available to you.

---

[27]   (2019) McGrath, Robert E. and Niemiec Ryan M., The Power of Character Strengths: Appreciate and Ignite Your Positive Personality, VIA Institute of Character pg. 203-209

Do You Have The Character Strength Of Creativity, Ingenuity, Or Originality?[2829]

According to Dictionary.com, having creativity means: "The ability to transcend traditional ideas, rules, patterns, relationships, or the like, and to create meaningful new ideas, forms, methods, interpretations, etc.; originality, progressiveness, or imagination." It takes a lot of creativity to write a book like this one. It is harder for me because I am not that creative and creativity is not a top strength of mine. I tend to be more structured and more adept at following established standards and rules that have already been proven to work in the past. On the other hand, my daughter is full of creativity and is a great artist and original thinker. I believe at some level we all have some form of ingenuity and originality if we are willing to search for it and find something we love doing and develop that skill as much as possible. Doing this will make us even more imaginative and will inspire us, which can improve our mind, body, and spirit over the course of our lifetime.

Knowing yourself and your character strengths, such as having creativity, has so many benefits, and if applied

---

28   https://www.dictionary.com/browse/creativity
29   ©Copyright 2004-2019, VIA Institute on Character. All Rights
      Reserved. Used with Permission. www.viacharacter.org

correctly, will make you feel like you have super powers because you will be working in your natural flow. In this way, we can build those strengths, which will then build self-confidence and self-awareness of one's own natural abilities. "Self-confidence and greater self-knowledge are byproducts of creativity that can help you feel comfortable in a variety of situations and adapt to challenges and stressors." (Niemiec and McGrath, 2019). So, therefore, challenge yourself to learn something new that will stretch and strengthen you. It will only make you better and stronger than you were before.

Know Your Strengths: Are You A Believer Of Fairness, Equity, And Justice For All?

"Fairness involves the belief that everyone's opinion counts, whether or not they share the same opinion." (Niemiec and McGrath, 2019[30]). The word "just" is an adjective which means guided by truth, reason, justice, and fairness. (Dictionary.com[31]) "Equity" is a noun and is defined as the quality of being fair or impartial. (Dictionary.com[32])

Having the character strengths of fairness, equity, and justice are very noble traits to embody because they are necessary for people in leadership such as Supreme Court Justices and others, like business owners who want to grow and prosper. I knew I had these character strengths early on as a teenager when I saw the injustices in the world.

I thought at the time I would go to college to become a criminal defense attorney because so many of my peers were going to jail and it just did not feel fair to me. After researching the industry and realizing it was such an overwhelming, mentally-challenging profession, I

---

[30] ©Copyright 2004-2019, VIA Institute on Character. All Rights
[31] https://www.dictionary.com/browse/just
[32] https://www.dictionary.com/browse/equity"

decided that maybe this type of work would not be a great fit for me. So, when it was time to go to college, I changed my major to Computer Information Systems and the res‾ is history. Little did I know, I would be fighting cybercrime today just as I originally wan‾ed to do in the past, just now in Cybersecurity.

As I mentioned earlier, fairness, equity, and justice also play a role in information technology because there are good and bad guys in this field. You need to decide what side you are going to represent because you will be entrusted with a lot of privileges and you need to be trustwor‾hy and have the utmost integrity if you want a successful career. All it takes is one wrorg turn into the dark side and you can tarnish your career forever. I believe it takes a certain type of person tc do this type of law-abiding work for the good and not be tempted to do bad things.

Please remember that all the great work you do now will pay off in the end when you are considered as a trusted expert and authority figure who is respected and looked up to for guidance and knowledge to protect the world's assets and future endeavors.

Know Your Strengths: Do You Have A Lot Of Curiosity And Interest In The World Around You?

One of the 24 Values in Action (VIA) character strengths is called curiosity. This is a trait I remember having as early as 2 years old or so. My family has told me for a long time that I have had this trait all this time. You may have heard the saying, the "terrible 2's". This is the age or time period when children start to develop more curiosity and hands-on experiences where they are more than likely getting into trouble, such as grabbing hold of dangerous things or things that may not be good for them to play with, mostly around the house or sometimes even out and about in public.

"To be curious is to explore and discover, to take an interest in ongoing experiences for its own sake... When you are at your best with curiosity, your mind is on fire with wonder and interest." (Neimiec and McGrath, 2019[33])

Having this curiosity trait has served me well for so many years in my personal encounters, my educational experiences, and now, as I coach my clients, in my current profession. If you have the curiosity characteristic,

---

[33] ©Copyright 2004-2019, VIA Institute on Character. All Rights Reserved. Used with Permission. www.viacharacter.org

know that it is a benefit and will serve you well in some strange and fascinating ways. Sometimes being a know-it-all is not good, but if you approach more things from a point of curiosity and are inquisitive, you open yourself to a more interesting world, and it makes for a more joyful and pleasant understanding. Do like a child does when they are trying to learn something new and go through life being more present and aware of the moment you are in. Then you will see and experience life more abundantly.

BREAKING
THE CYBER CODE

Know Your Strengths: Do You Have The Virtue Of Spirituality?

"As a character strength, spirituality involves the belief that there is a dimension to life that is beyond human understanding. Some people don't connect this belief with the concept of divinity and prefer to think of it in terms of sense of meaning rather than spirituality, but in the VIA Classification the terms are considered closely related." (Niemiec & McGrath, 2019[34])

Spirituality is one of my top 8 VIA Character Strengths. I use this virtue in many ways, especially during challenging and stressful times in my life when I do not understand why certain things are happening to me or even when the world around me seems negative and difficult to handle.

Do not get spirituality confused with the practice of religion or being religious because they have different meanings. For example, being religious may be something like going to church every Sunday or practicing daily prayer several times a day. Spirituality is how we find meaning in our everyday lives and how we understand the way things work in the universe around us.

There cre times in my deep despair when I ask myself, "Why is this certain situation happening right now?" Later I realize there had to be a reason for that very thing to happer to me and my spiritual way of thinking about it soothes my soul. I try to find comfort in those hard times by tellirg myself everything happens for a reason and what is just is, and that tends to relieve some of the pain in that moment.

There cre times that spirituality can be overused or underused, so try to find the right balance and not overly offend anyone with your ways of handling things with spirituali-y. Spirituality can help you get through the tough times, sc by all means, make it a daily, weekly, or monthly ritual to do something that makes your inner being happier because everyone around you will definitely be better off that you did this for yourself.

BREAKING
THE CYBER CODE

Do I Have The Superpower Character Strengths Of Zest, Enthusiasm, And Energy?

"Zest means approaching a situation, or life in general, with excitement and energy, not approaching tasks or activities halfway or halfheartedly. The character strength of zest is related to vitality, which comes from the Latin word vita, meaning life." (Niemiec and McGrath, 2019[35]).

Zest is a very powerful innate strength to have, and for me it is not in my top10 traits because energy for me is sometimes hard to come by. For those who do have it as a top10 strength, it can be an amazing thing to see in action. Having enthusiasm for life is something I want everyone to have and experience as much as humanly possible because we are all deserving of life and of being here on this planet. So, enjoy life every chance you get with appreciation for what you do have going for you as much as you can. This world can be hard to deal with at times, so this strength can go a very long way in helping us cope on those extremely challenging days.

Sometimes though, our enthusiasm and energy for things can be underused or overused in certain peculiar situations, so we must be mindful of when it is most appropriate to show this strength to others. Zest is very beneficial when it comes to things like overall health and well-being. We will tend to be more conscientious of what works best to boost that very energy which will cause us to be more proactive at doing those things that enhance or energize us because they make us feel so much better.

For some people, we may need to pay more attention to those times when our energy levels are being depleted or when we are dissatisfied with something that is draining us. We may need to find ways to get back that enthusicsm for life so we can then enjoy more and thrive. Remember we all lose enthusiasm at some point and sometimes that is okay, just do not stay down and live there if you can do something about it.

Knowing Your Strengths: Are You A Grateful Person Who Tries To See The Blessing In Many Things?

"Grateful people experience a variety of positive emotions, and those emotions inspire them to act in more virtuous ways—humbler, more persistent, or kinder." (Niemiec and McGrath, 2019[36])

Gratitude has been a top character strength of mine for a very long time. It is in my absolute best interests for my brain health to be grateful since I have been blessed with so many opportunities over my lifetime. Let's be clear: there are times and situations that have happened to me in the past that I have wondered, why me, but overall, eventually those things worked out for my good or were lessons learned.

I have a ritual I practice where I write five things every Sunday night that happened during that week for which I am grateful. It is always so amazing to look back on what I have recorded in my journal over several weeks and months to see and experience how blessed I was for these things to happen to me. If you are not the type of person who counts your blessings on a regular basis, you should give it a try because the happiness and warmth it brings and the resulting positive emotions will uplift your entire situation in that very moment.

As a result of my gratefulness, I have become a warmer and kinder person and have more empathy for others. That is such a wonderful character trait to have during challenging times. So, humble yourself and realize that you are a uniquely-designed, special person who is here for a reason, and that reason is to make a difference in this world. There is no one like you in this entire world who has all the quality traits and the skill set you have developed, so be thankful for this life and make the best of every opportunity you get to make an impact on someone else's life.

Please remember, there will be challenges, but they will make you stronger and better than before, so share your brilliance and shine bright in this life wherever you go.

Know Your Strengths: Spreading Kindness And Generosity

"Kindness is being with others, giving your time, money, and talents to support those in need... Kindness is also being nurturing and caring to others—to enjoy doing favors for them, to take care of them, and to perform good deeds." (Niemiec and McGrath, 2019[37])

I am generally a kind and generous person because I remember many times in the past when I did not have the means for food, shelter, and clothes, being in a low-income family and single-parent household. So, as a result, we had to turn to charity organizations, friends, and family just to make it through the day. Thankfully and gratefully, these people and organizations had a giving heart and believed in giving of themselves, their time, and their precious resources; otherwise, my family and I would have had to do without the necessities, struggling to stay alive. Fortunately, as of the writing of this book, my family and I are doing so much better overall, and now I am in a place to share of myself to help future cybersecurity professionals.

---

[37] ©Copyright 2004-2019, VIA Institute on Character. All Rights Reserved. Used with Permission. www.viacharacter.org

There are many times when kindness and generosity can be overused and, in those times, we need to reflect and determine if what we are providing is really being appreciated. There have been times where I have given of my time and money and other support systems, and it was taken for granted and I was upset because of the wasted resources and ungratefulness that I experienced. I just chalked it up as a gift that would eventually come back to me in a different way when I least expected it. Do not get me wrong: you should not give expecting something in return, but you should make sure you are able to take care of your own needs and make sure you can sustain yourself in the event of an emergency or unexpected downturn.

The act of generosity makes me incredibly happy and fills my cup with gratitude and cheer because I know it will make a difference someway somehow. Keep giving with no strings attached and you will be graced with unexpected blessings and joy when you least expect it. I realize that if no one had cared or invested in me and my family, I may have not been here today to share my story of resilience.

BREAKING
THE CYBER CODE

Knowing Your Strengths: Are Honesty, Authenticity, And Genuineness Part Of Your Character?

"When you are honest, you speak the truth. More broadly, you present yourself in a genuine and sincere way, without pretense, and taking responsibility for your feelings and actions." (Niemiec and McGrath, 2019[38]).

It takes a special type of person to be honest and forthcoming about how they feel and what they believe in and value. But, some people will not appreciate this type of person's candor because they may not be ready to deal with the reality of the situation to appreciate the truth. There may even be times when it is simply easier to sugarcoat things and be sensitive to the needs of others so that there are no bad feelings. It is important to value other people's feelings on certain matters, so beware of full openness. There may be other times when people will really appreciate your realness and frankness. They will look for you to tell it like it is and give them the best constructive criticism there is, so they can learn, grow, and improve their current circumstances. These may be your kind of people.

---

[38] ©Copyright 2004-2019, VIA Institute on Character. All Rights Reserved. Used with Permission. www.viacharacter.org

Be careful if it is your significant other or a trusted friend or family member who cannot handle the truth. You may get yourself in trouble because sometimes your truthful insight can be painful and hard to deal with; even worse, it may affect the well-being and happiness of those whom you love and cherish the most. Either way, honesty, authenticity, and genuineness can be refreshing at times, but you need to be intentionally mindful and artful because it is a delicate balancing act to be so forthcoming all the time. However, authentic is an incredibly beautiful place to be in your life, and knowing thyself is always a benefit to you. It can take some people several years to get to the point of trusting themselves and sharing their own thoughts with the world. Own this wonderful character strength and use it wisely because it is an extremely strong attribute to cultivate.

Knowing Your Strength: Have You Demonstrated Bravery Or Valor In Your Life?

"Bravery comes in at least three forms. There is the physical form, when you take risks with your body, which is demonstrated by soldiers and firefighters. There is the psychological form, which occurs when you face your own mental, emotional, and other personal problems directly. A third form of bravery is moral, to speak up for what is right even if there is opposition." (Niemiec & McGrath, 2019[39])

If you examine your past experiences, you may discover there were times in your life where you had to be brave and face a situation head on, even when you did not know the consequences of that bravery.

I personally have not served in the military nor been a police officer or firefighter, but there was definitely bravery in having my first child because the thought occurred to me one day during my pregnancy that a child would have to come out of my body whether I was ready or not. Childbirth is very risky for mothers and it can be a life and death situation for some. I knew I had to prepare for that day and be ready for anything that

---

[39] ©Copyright 2004-2019, VIA Institute on Character. All Rights Reserved. Used with Permission. www.viacharacter.org

might occur. It turned out to be an incredibly stressful delivery because the umbilical cord was wrapped around my newborn's neck inside me and I had to have an immediate caesarian section to save my daughter's life because she could not breathe. I was so scared, that while on the delivery table with all my doctors surrounding me, I broke out into a Mariah Carey song (*Vision of Love*) to ease the fear of the delivery and possibly to guide my daughter out with my voice, so she could come into this world safe and sound. Well, it worked and I ended up having a happy, healthy, 8 lbs. 6 oz. baby girl on Mother's Day 2005. The rest is now history.

Another form of bravery I have tried to practice is the psychological, mental, and emotional stamina to face my fears in order to take the necessary action to achieve any career and life goals that I once dreamed of, through all the obstacles that were placed in front of me, from the time I was in college to this day. I had to search deep down inside to find the necessary courage and valor to beat the odds stacked against me. It was very taxing and mentally draining to face discrimination, gender bias, and poverty to get to where I am today, but I did it and I lived to tell this story.

Finally, the last form of bravery is moral, and it is what keeps me going. Equality, justice, financial freedom, liberty, and fairness are some of the things I strive to achieve for the youth coming behind me who want to succeed in building a better life for themselves and their families. I believe it is a worthy cause to want to leave this world a little better than you found it, and that is what strengthens me every day to want to continue sharing and building up others.

BREAKING
THE CYBER CODE

Know Your Strengths: How Citizenship, Teamwork, And Loyalty Are Demonstrated

"Teamwork extends to being a good citizen of your community or country, and more broadly to a sense of social responsibility for particular groups of people or even all humanity. In other words, the person high in teamwork applies a certain way of acting in whatever context they consider themselves committed to the good of the group as a whole. Most commonly, however, this strength refers to your being a dedicated, reliable, and contributing member to your small group or team." (Niemiec & McGrath, 2019[40])

As a teenager, I played junior varsity basketball and was an average player, but I was a great on defense and shared the ball with the better members on the team who could make the best plays in order to win the game. I did not realize at the time that I was learning teamwork, leadership, loyalty, conflict resolution, and other team-building exercises that would help me be a better basketball player, student, employee, business owner, family member, and friend later in life. In addition, I learned years ago that citizenship is an important aspect of being an American, and I recognized that even more

---

when I voted in my very first presidential election in 1996. I remember seeing past stories of how my black ancestors struggled to gain the right to vote and why it meant so much more to me to exercise that very right and privilege to vote and support the causes and people who I believed could make a difference in my community and in the nation.

I later understood that I thrive more when working in team environments. I always try to aim for consensus and want everyone to have a say in the outcome so that the project or initiative we are embarking on better succeeds at its mission and is more successful because everyone participated. In the past, I have taken on too much responsibility as a team member and later was resentful because others were slacking off or just were not real willing or able to work as a team player and pull their own weight. I had to learn not to overwork myself and even better spread out the tasks more fairly while also prioritizing the assignments so that I did not burn myself out and regret the entire thing.

It is extremely important to know your limits and understand what you bring to the table, because some people may not always put in the work. Remember to look out for yourself and your mental well-being in order to manage the workload equally. I discovered a long time ago the hard way that when I am passionate about something, I can overdo it and that is not good for me or anyone else. Understand your value and know what skills you bring to the effort because teamwork succeeds when everyone plays a role in the outcome.

Know Your Strengths: Why Having Hope, Optimism, And Future-Mindedness Is Key

"Having the character strength of hope and optimism is more than a feel-good emotion; it is an action-oriented strength involving agency and the motivation and confidence that goals can be reached. Hope is anchored in the present, in the understanding of where things are now, but is sailing toward the future." (Niemiec & McGrath, 2019[41])

I remember when I first started to pursue a career in Information Technology, I was so full of hope and optimism for all the future possibilities to share my new-found knowledge by helping the businesses that I worked for solve the Y2K issue in the late 1990's. I was a little naïve to the fact that I was going to be turned down from getting those jobs just because I was a new college graduate with just an associate degree and was a double minority who had not proven herself yet. Moreover, I was passionate and full of hope, and I thought that would be enough for someone to give me a chance. I later found out after numerous tries that this

---

would not be the case and was extremely disappointed and discouraged to the point of giving up.

I almost quit the industry entirely and was thinking of denying myself my dream to work in the technology industry. It did not help that we were approaching the dot-com bubble that would devastate the whole industry. but I was determined and fearless and a little immature to think that a business would take a risk and hire me at this uncertain turbulent time period. So, I postponed my quest to join the industry until there were better days to come for this promising career field of the future. Ultimately, with the education I gained in college, I managed to use those same skills I'd learned to implement computer information systems infrastructures in my subsequent careers as a real estate agent, retail manager, and restaurant owner, and was surprised that these new abilities would be so beneficial and transferable across different fields and job functions and truly cross-functional. I later learned these skills would be needed all the time and everywhere. After realizing this knowledge would not go to waste and these valuable skills were useful no matter where I landed, I started feeling more confident about my different work experiences, even though I was not in an official technology role.

I later used those on-the-job learning skills and projects to beef up my resume and continued to apply for those technology roles. Eventually, I started getting call backs and interviews because companies wanted to learn more about my skills. My future seemed brighter every day. I am so happy that I never lost hope and I finally did get my first computer technician role of my dreams.

Know Your Strengths: What Does It Mean To Have Perseverance Despite The Odds

"Perseverance is sticking with things. It means being hardworking and finishing what is started, despite barriers and obstacles that arise." (Niemiec and McGrath, 2019[42])

I could have been a statistic because I came from a low-income, single-parent household and was faced with violence and stress most of my early life. I lost my only brother to gun violence in 2000 and that could have been me too. I knew from an incredibly young age, as the oldest of five siblings, that I had to be a leader and example for the ones coming up behind me. As soon as I was old enough to get a job, I did and started making money at 12 years old with my paper route. My sister tagged along with me as I wanted her to see the possibilities of making your own way by being responsible and taking the initiative to provide for yourself.

I always believed I deserved a better life, and when given the chance, I could go after my dreams and make something of myself so I could help my mother and the rest of my entire family. I was always curious and loved to learn and grow, so I enjoyed school a lot and even team

---

[42]   ©Copyright 2004-2019, VIA Institute on Character. All Rights Reserved. Used with Permission. www.viacharacter.org

sports. I did not realize at the time that my intelligence would lead me to obtain 4 college degrees and several industry certifications, but here I am today. I am saying all this to say, it took so much strength and perseverance that there were times when I wanted to give up and just be average, because no one around me was trying as hard as I was to achieve these tremendously hard goals, and it was lonely and unbearable. I was up against biases, discrimination, and racism, and still I wanted to keep going.

I did not know it then, but I know it now, that I was being guided by a higher power bigger than myself that I could lean on when times got tough. When you are faced with huge odds, you need a support system to lean on. You will want to quit and that will seem like the best thing to do at the time, but it will not be. You will have to dig deep and remember your purpose and why you originally set out to achieve these goals. Take time every chance you get to reflect, adjust, and reset. When that is done, get back to work and finish what you started, because in the end, you will be extremely proud of yourself and all the hard work you put in. No one will be able to take away your achievements and accomplishments. and that will be a powerful place to be.

Know Your Strengths: How Essential Is Judgment, Critical Thinking, And Open-Mindedness?

"Judgment involves making rational and logical choices, and analytically evaluating ideas, opinions, and facts. Judgment also involves being open-minded and able to change one's mind in the light of evidence, remaining open to other arguments and perspectives." (Niemiec and McGrath, 2019[43])

Judgment, critical thinking skills, and being open-minded are essential character traits to have because there are so many difficult issues in this world, and it will take these types of abilities to solve these pressing problems. I remember my early years when I did not have to use these strengths because my family did the thinking for me and I had to settle for what they thought was best for me. It was not until I decided to go to college and pay my own way that I had the opportunity to choose my own pathway in my career and my life. I realize now that I probably did not have enough knowledge to pick the right choices back then. Now, having a child of my own, I realize I have been choosing what I believe is best for her and that will not always be the case. That is why I am

---

doing my best to lead by example by helping her find diverse careers in Science, Technology, Engineering, and Mathematics (STEM) jobs because these are the careers of the future and are high-paying for professionals, such as Information Technology, Artificial Intelligence, Data Scientist, and many of the Engineering disciplines which are merging STEM concepts in every profession in the 21st century. Math is also a very important skillset because you need to have accounting to know how to write a check, balance your bank account, pay your bills on time, and pay taxes, to name a few.

We all need critical thinking skills to pick the right opportunities in our everyday lives while also being careful to judge others fairly and with an open mind because none of us are perfect human beings. I am saying all of this to say that we need to use our minds purposefully and strategically, so when we are faced with tough situations, we take care to be deliberate and smart about our decisions the majority of the time.

BREAKING
THE CYBER CODE

Know Your Strengths: Do You Have The Character Quality Of Leadership

"As a character strength, leadership refers to the tendency to organize and encourage a group to get things done while maintaining good relations within the group. Effective leaders are able to provide a positive vision or message that inspires dedicated followers who feel empowered and perhaps even inspired." (Niemiec and McGrath, 2019[44])

I do not know if you are a believer in natural-born leaders or if you are a believer that leaders are made, but I was the firstborn of five children and I had to naturally take the lead and be an example for my siblings—whether I wanted to or not. Do not get me wrong, you can always learn and improve in the leadership arena, but some things are just out of your control and you just need to step up and take the lead.

I admire and look up to people who have strong leadership skills in integrity, fairness, communication, and ethics, and who also have great critical-thinking abilities because everyone around them benefits from this type of leader. Leadership skills have the potential to take you

---

44   ©Copyright 2004-2019, VIA Institute on Character. All Rights Reserved. Used with Permission. www.viacharacter.org

into higher trusted circles of influence that are beyond what you can only dream. Leadership can be developed by taking the necessary actions and not being too afraid to take the required measures to move forward on the goals and plans you want to achieve.

As an aspiring leader, always remember to continuously learn and to develop yourself every day. It does not mean you must be a know-it-all, but it does mean you need to be ready and willing to try something new and be courageous. There are definitely a lot of things I want to do in this life that will take some initiative and a little more bravery, but I am willing to prepare and push myself to take the necessary actions on those things when the time is right. We all have this one life, and we need to learn and grow and be willing to make mistakes so we can benefit from the lessons learned and share our experiences with others so they will know what is possible.

This is one of the reasons I do what I do and why I wrote this book, because I wanted the next generation behind me to know the skills, qualities, abilities, character traits, and tools needed to get ahead and make their dreams a reality. If I had never tried and failed before, I never would have met any of my goals and dreams of today. So, keep dreaming, thinking, planning, and doing what it takes to get what you deserve in life, and never quit on yourself. There are so many people out there who are counting on you to win.

BREAKING
THE CYBER CODE

Know Your Strengths: Do You Have A Passion And A Love For Learning New Things?

"Love of learning refers to the desire to hold on to and deepen information. If you love to learn, the reading of one blog post or hearing a two-sentence response to your question is not enough for you." (Niemiec and McGrath, 2019[45])

I know this to be true because I wear my character strength for the love of learning as a badge of honor. It has gotten me through several college degrees and certification tracks that were so challenging and difficult to obtain that I almost wanted to give up. Instead, my love of learning helped me to be more curious, to not be afraid to fail, and to get back up again to finish what I had started. There are times when my love of learning causes me to overdo it and leads me into a never-ending spiral of information overload that is hard to control to get out of the cycle of interesting details. It is at this time that I try to stop, reassess the information I have already gained, then try to make the best-guess effort on the

---

facts so I can take the next step and act on that information.

With the advent of the Internet, there are now such vast amounts of data and information everywhere and all around us that it can be overwhelming just to try to decide what to do. When this happens, it is best to take a breather, re-evaluate, and make the best decision you can. Additionally, having the strength of the love of learning has many health and well-being benefits that I believe everyone should try to integrate in our lives as much as possible so that our minds are refreshed and renewed each and every day.

I read a lot of books and watch intriguing news stories and documentaries as a hobby out of curiosity so that I have more knowledge and facts to share with others I meet in new networking opportunities and also with my friends and family. Research has shown that our brains are elastic and can stretch and grow with new connections based off learning new details and facts, so we can and should try to learn more. Just remember to not overdo it and get lost in all the fascinating facts. Take some dedicated time to reflect and find new ways to share that information to help you and others become better individuals who are more aware and knowledgeable of the world around us.

Know Your Strengths: How Does Having Humility And Being Humble Help Us?

"Truly humble people think well of themselves and have a good sense of who they are, but they also are aware of their mistakes, gaps in their knowledge, and imperfections. Most importantly, they are content without being a center of attention or getting praised for their accomplishments." (Niemiec and McGrath, 2019[46])

There are many reasons a person becomes humble, due to either crises or challenges that we may have experienced or other circumstances beyond our control. It is not a bad thing to be a humble person. I remember more recently during the 2008 and 2009 recession that I almost lost everything and had to humbly re-invent my lifestyle and career. It can happen to the best of us. We think we are on top of the world, and something devasting happens and wipes all our gains away overnight. With every adversity, there are lessons to be learned. You can get through it and come out even better for it, stronger and more resilient in your efforts.

We as human being are realizing that we need others to share their weaknesses, obstacles, and successes so we know it is possible to get through the difficulties in our lives. I feel more comfortable around the more authentic, transparent person who is not afraid to be honest and forthcoming with information because then I am in a much better place to make the best decision with the situation at hand.

We can and should be confident and sure of our abilities, but we need to understand that we all have gaps in our knowledge and skills in some areas. That is okay because we will never be perfect in everything we do. Become aware of what your limitations are and work on improving what is possible. Know that we will make mistakes, but we can make improvements and progress on those things if we are willing to do the work. I have had to humble myself my entire career and there may be times where you may have to do the same.

Know Your Strengths: Consider The Perspective In Your Everyday Situations[47]

"Perspective means the ability to see the bigger picture in life. This is the ability to look at systems as a whole, or to think in big terms, which helps you to offer good advice." (Niemiec & McGrath, 2019)

A person who tries to look at all sides of an issue and consider the bigger picture comes up with a better solution in almost any situation. There are certainly times when we feel our perspective is the only one that is right, but that is not the whole picture. We all have diverse life experiences, causing us to see things a little differently from someone else, which may not be right or wrong but is just our perspective and the way we see things.

There have been so many times when I thought I was totally justified in a certain situation—until I listened to someone else's side of the story and it was also valid. I believe we could solve a lot of the world's current problems if we just would consider all sides of an issue before making a life-changing decision that also will affect others. Having perspective of a situation is extremely valuable and is the smart thing to do so we can choose a better option. That is why, before I make a

---

tough decision, I ask others around me for their feedback and opinions just so I may get some clarity or be shown something I may have missed. Our own judgments may be flawed. Therefore, sometimes other people's perspectives are helpful so we can choose wisely with the most information possible and the best facts available. We will be better off knowing the most about the situation. Face it: we cannot possibly know everything. We need to choose our people wisely so we get the best details about the subject matter.

Remember also to trust your instincts and intuition because you may have knowledge of a similar situation that may help you make a wiser choice. In the end, our own perspective should be the most valuable choice because, ultimately, we will be the one who has to live with all the choices we make. So, always remember to believe in your own judgement too.

BREAKING
THE CYBER CODE

Know Your Strength: How Good Are You At Self-Control And Self-Regulation?

"The mantra of the self-regulated person is that you know when 'enough is enough'. When you are at your best with self-regulation, you exercise discipline and self-control with your health habits, emotions, and impulses, while allowing yourself spontaneous pleasures and staying reasonably flexible in you daily routines." (Niemiec & McGrath, 2019[48])

I will be honest with you, I struggle a lot with self-control and self-regulation because sometimes I act on impulse, which is not always the best thing to do. I would call myself a "work in progress" when it comes to self-discipline, and lately, I have been getting better at it because I have made a deliberate effort to be intentional with working on my self-control. I decided to start small by having a daily routine to get some exercise every day and I have a daily ritual to write in my journal at the end of the evening about things I am grateful for. I also told myself that I need to be more mindful of what I put in my body when it comes to my diet. I am not perfect, but I have gotten better, especially when I tend

---

to track my progress in my activity tracker. Like I said, I am a work n progress because sometimes I get annoyed at the daily activity tracker and stop logging in it altogether because it seems so controlling and tedious. It also forces me to see how bad or good I am doing, so it can make me feel bad when progress is not being made. This is my constant struggle with self-discipline, and it frustrates me because I like to go with my feelings and gut instincts and do what I want when I want, which is the part of the problem, right?

Self-regulation is a great quality to have because it can help you achieve monumental things. I have been disciplined when it comes to my education and career goals, which I would say have benefitted me greatly, but I want to work more on having healthy habits and that is my biggest challenge right now. We all have something we need to work on, and it is important not to be too hard on yourself and just try doing the best you can every single day. I will find the self- control I need to make the best choices every chance I get, and I hope you do too.

BREAKING
THE CYBER CODE

Know Your Strengths: Have You Ever Demonstrated Social Intelligence Skills?

"When a person knows what makes other people tick, he or she is displaying social intelligence. They can feel comfortable and say the right thing whether they're in the boardroom or the janitorial room, in a school setting or at a construction site." (Niemiec and McGrath, 2019[49])

For me, social intelligence skills are a work in progress because in my early years there was no filter on what came out my mouth. I either would be too shy and say nothing and let things go the way the other person wanted things to go, or I would say something that did not make sense and feel like an idiot afterward. These days, I have learned how to be mindful of what and how I do things by thinking about the other person's feelings before I take an action or say something I will regret. That takes a lot of practice.

What I have learned is that it is sometimes better to keep your thoughts to yourself if it will not improve the situation. I know there are people who will not take a second to think about how their words and actions could affect

---

[49]   ©Copyright 2004-2019, VIA Institute on Character. All Rights Reserved. Used with Permission. www.viacharacter.org

others. I have been on the other end of those conversations and it is an uncomfortable feeling. I don't want my actions to hurt someone else, so I try to incorporate social intelligence skills and some empathy when interacting with people I care about.

You must want to be better to develop these social intelligence skills, and I am still learning how to do this every day. When I see how these skills improve my overall relationships at home and at work, it is priceless. We could all benefit if we try to put ourselves in the place of others and think before we speak. There would be better workplaces, better negotiations, peace, and better friendships all around the world if we worked at these necessary skills. As a result of some training on crucial conversations and individual positive psychology coaching, I have improved a lot in my days. I hope you will find the time one day to want to improve your encounters by building and developing your social intelligence skills too.

Why Taking A Personality Assessment Is Important For Your Life And Career

When I first started out, I did not know a lot of about personality assessments even though all throughout grade school we took all kinds of assessments. At the time, I did not realize that these assessments were important for my progress and advancement to the next level. I believe I did not realize it until I went to see a career advisor who told me she wanted me to take an assessment to find out my interest and values, and even then, it did not dawn on me that the potential outcome could decide my destiny.

There are three personality assessments that I have become very intrigued with over the years, and these are the VIA Character Assessment[50], Gallup's Clifton Strengths[51] Finder, and Myers-Briggs Type Indicator[52] assessments. Each assessment has its uniqueness and can be used in all kinds of fascinating ways. Be mindful that they may not be totally "the end all/be all" for accuracy,

---

[50] https://www.viacharacter.org/personality-assessments
[51] https://www.gallup.com/cliftonstrengths/en/253715/34-cliftonstrengths-themes.aspx
[52] https://www.myersbriggs.org/my-mbti-personality-type/mbti-basics/

but these assessments tend to be extremely helpful in identifying very closely your true personality traits.

"The VIA Character Survey is a psychometrically-validated personality test that measures an individual's character strengths. Character strengths are viewed as our positive personality in that they are our core capacities for thinking, feeling, and behaving in ways that can bring benefit to oneself and others. We express our character strengths universally across all domains—work, relationships, school, social, etc."

"The purpose of the Myers-Briggs Type Indicator® (MBTI®) personality inventory is to make the theory of psychological types described by C. G. Jung understandable and useful in people's lives. The essence of the theory is that much seemingly-random variation in the behavior is actually quite orderly and consistent, being due to basic differences in the ways individuals prefer to use their perception and judgment."

"When you take the Clifton Strength Finder assessment, you uncover your unique combination of 34 Clifton Strengths themes. The themes, which sort into four domains, are a culmination of decades led by Don Clifton of research to study and categorize the talents of the world's most successful people. Together, the themes explain a simple but profound element of human behavior: what's *right* with people."

All three of these assessments have been extremely beneficial in me understanding myself better and in choosing the right opportunities in my personal life and career. I believe everyone can benefit from taking a personality assessment so we can understand ourselves better at a deeper level than the eyes can see. If you are not sure about these types of tests, then that is fine too because you may know yourself better than anyone else and these types of tests may be strange to you. In that case, you may want to ask your family and friends what they think about your personality and character traits in order to get a more accurate viewpoint of your strengths.

Free And Low-Cost Online Cybersecurity Learning Content Listed By N.I.C.E.[53]

1. Center for Development of Security Excellence Cybersecurity eLearning

   "Free cybersecurity eLearning courses for the *Department of Defense (DoD) and other U.S. government personnel and contractors* within the National Industrial Security Program (NISP)."

2. Chief Information Security Officer (CISO) Workshop Training

   "Training provided by Microsoft that includes a collection of security learnings, principles, and recommendations for modernizing security in your organization."

3. Critical Knowledge Explorer

   "CyberVista offering that includes more than 22 hours of free on-demand training and discounted labs covering Network Fundamentals, Threats and Attacks, and Network Security."

---

[53] https://www.nist.gov/itl/applied-cybersecurity/nice/resources/online-learning-content

4.   Cyberbit Range Remote Training

"Free remote training for SOC teams, providing live, simulated cyberattacks on Cyberbit's cloud-based Cyber Range."

5.   Cyber Training 365 Online Academy

"Free courses and *low-cost* subscriptions to help you master cybersecurity techniques such as Analyzing Malware, Penetration Testing, Advanced Persistent Threats, and much more. A low-cost lifetime subscription is also available."

6.   Cybrary

"Free information technology and cybersecurity training portal."

BREAKING
THE CYBER CODE

Why Science, Technology, Engineering, And Mathematics (STEM) College Degrees?[54]

"The Bureau of Labor Statistics (BLS) projects a 12% growth in computer and information technology occupations from 2018 to 2028. A computer science degree can lead to a variety of careers, depending on the individual's specialty and education level. An associate degree provides the fastest path to entry-level positions in areas such as programming and information security. A bachelor's degree can qualify degree-holders for careers in system architecture, network and database management, and electrical engineering. Specialized leadership and research positions generally require a master's degree or doctorate. Graduates with an advanced degree often pursue roles in systems analysis, hardware and software development, and postsecondary education.[55]"

I am passionate about Science, Technology, Engineering, and Math (STEM) because these subjects are so fascinating, wonderous, innovative, inspiring, and have so much growth

---

[54] https://careerwise.minnstate.edu/careers/stemcareers
https://www.valuecolleges.com/degrees/science-technology-mathematics-engineering/
https://www.collegechoice.net/faq/what-kinds-of-degrees-are-available-in-computers-and-technology/

[55] (www.Collegechoice.net)

potential now and for the foreseeable future. This is one of the biggest reasons why I started my company, STEM Coaching, LLC, so I could share my knowledge and expertise and advocate for youths to go after these high-paying careers because they can change their lives and their financial statuses for the better. There are numerous careers in STEM, such as biology, nuclear science, accounting, astrology, computers, aviation, and so many more that I cannot begin to list them all.

In the United States, leaders are advocating that students should be taught about these subjects and learn about STEM careers as early as elementary school, so they will be better prepared to enter into these job markets right after college and they can land a good-paying position immediately. As a mother of a young teenager, I have taken it upon myself at every opportunity to expose my daughter to Science, Technology, Engineering, and Math courses as early as age seven. Now she is very capable of the advanced content in high school, and hopefully, will be for college one day. If you have the opportunity to learn these topics in grade school, in your local community, or even in college, I believe it will greatly expand your career choices and better your life for years to come.

More Self-Study Books To Help You Build Your Cybersecurity Career Today[56]

In the cybersecurity career field, there is a need to continuously stay on top of your knowledge, skills, abilities, and the trends. There are new threats and challenges every day, and you want to be informed, be your best, and be prepared each time. Below I have recommended some additional self-help books to get you on your way to upskilling yourself and getting more expertise in cybersecurity.

Book Recommendations:[57]

1.   *Cybersecurity for Beginners* by Raef Meeuwise (2017)

2.   *Hacking for Dummies* (Computer/Tech) by Kevin Beaver (2018)

3.   *Networking All-In-One for Dummies* by Doug Lowe (2020)

4.   *Social Engineering: The Science of Human Hacking* by Christopher Hadnagy (2018)

5.   *CompTIA Security + Get Certified Get Ahead* by Darryl Gibson (2017)

---

[56]   https://cybersecuritycoursesonline.com/top-10-books-for-beginners-learning-cybersecurity/

[57]   https://bookauthority.org/books/beginner-cyber-security-books

6. *(ISC)2 CISSP Official Study Guide and Practice Test Bundle* by Mike Chapple

7. *Cybersecurity for Executives: A Practical Guide* by Gregory Touhill (2014)

8. *Security Operations Center: Building, Operating, and Maintaining Your SOC by Munz, McIntyre, Alfarden* (2015)

9. *Threat Modeling: Designing for Security* by Adam Shostack (2014)

10. *The Cybersecurity to English Dictionary* by Raef Meeuwise (2018)

Remember to network and join industry associations so you can be informed of the latest education and information in the field. Strive to improve on your skills and abilities every chance you get. Stay curious and open-minded to new information that you have not considered before. This may very well be your advantage over others who are not as prepared as you. Once you have received your industry certifications, persist in acquiring continuing education credits and maintain them so they don't expire.

Research and advocate for credible resources and news outlets that will keep you abreast of the new technologies and innovative products coming on the market that you can possibly get a better understanding on and get training and additional knowledge on, so you can inform your organization and surrounding community.

Finally, I always advocate for higher education, so if you have the will to get a more advanced college degree, such as a master's degree if you don't already have one, that would be an awesome addition for your credibility and expertise.

BREAKING
THE CYBER CODE

Preparing For Situation, Task, Action, Result (STAR) Based Interviewing Responses[58]

"The STAR interview method is a technique you can use to prepare for behavioral and situational interview questions. STAR stands for: **Situation, Task, Action,** and **Result.** This method will help you prepare clear and concise responses using real-life examples. The STAR method helps you create an easy-to-follow story with a clear conflict and resolution." (www.indeed.com)[59]

First listen to the question and think of the event. Here is what each part of the technique means:

1. Situation: Describe the context within which you performed a job or faced a challenge at work.

2. Task: Describe your responsibility in that situation.

3. Action: Describe how you completed the task or endeavored to meet the challenge.

4. Result: Explain the outcomes or results generated by the action taken.

---

[58]   https://www.thebalancecareers.com/what-is-the-star-interview-response-technique-2061629
[59]   https://www.indeed.com/career-advice/interviewing/how-to-use-the-star-interview-response-technique

Since you will not know the types of questions the interviewer will ask in advance, you should prepare beforehand by thinking about all your previous work, education, or volunteer experiences. Then write all the scenarios out one-by-one on paper of how you will respond to them in the STAR format. Go online and research STAR-based-interview question types, so you get more ideas of how to answer these types of questions. The more you practice writing out everything, the more confident you will be at the time of the interview. You will be amazed at how concise you will be after doing your homework and will be better able to nail that interview. Good luck!

BREAKING
THE CYBER CODE

How Do You Combat Stress So You Can Have A Successful Career And Life?

As I write this book, the world is going through a once-in-a-lifetime pandemic called the Coronavirus. It has been devasting and the death toll has been enormous. This crisis has tested us all, and it has caused a lot of emotional and psychological damage that is still mounting. I must use my character strength of hope and spirituality to stay positive at this time, but it has not been easy at all. Recently, there was news that there are some medical breakthroughs coming soon, and medical professionals are predicting there may be an end to the pandemic in sight. I am excited and grateful for all the people involved in making things happen to improve this enormous health crisis—and as a result, the economic crisis of the healthcare industry—and for all the frontline workers who keep us going. We are stronger as community when we all work together to beat this thing.

Another crisis we are dealing with is an epidemic in the cybersecurity industry, which is one of the reasons I wrote this book The shortage of staff to fill these roles is complicated and has many reasons, more than people lacking the knowledge, skills, and abilities to do the job. The biggest reason is employers are not on the same page of the job requirements and job descriptions, and are posting jobs that are turning otherwise-eligible candidates away. There needs to be a standardized terminology, like the National Initiative of Cybersecurity Education (NICE) workforce framework used to create the appropriate roles for each job function.

Another issue is the current staff is being overworked and burned out, which is creating a toxic environment and causing health issues and people to eventually leave the company. Finally, another issue is work and life balance. It can be impossible to be on call 24/7 and have a family life too. So many other things are suffering as a result, such as sleep and productivity. All this is to say that these and other issues are making it hard for individuals and businesses to fight cybercrime, and be healthy and happy too.

An online article written by Jasmine Henry on the blog Security Intelligence reported these statistics on burnout of cybersecurity team members:[60]

- More than twice as likely to report poor work-life balance
  (44 percent vs. 20 percent);

- More than five times as likely to worry about job security
  (32 percent vs. 6 percent);

- More than three times as likely not to take full vacation days
  (89 percent vs. 28 percent).

---

[60] https://securityintelligence.com/articles/9-reasons-why-cybersecurity-stress-is-an-industry-epidemic/

If these types of statistics continue, the world could become a more unsafe place for companies and individuals who want to protect their sensitive information, such as financial data and health care information. I even considered leaving the industry when it got so bad in one environment. I then had to re-evaluate the situation and get some additional countermeasures in place because it was a very unhealthy place to work. As a result, I have made it my mission to improve the working environments around me where I live, work, and play, so the next individual or leader who comes behind me has a better, more positive, more inviting environment to thrive and succeed.

There are ways we can combat stress in this pandemic, stress in our jobs, and stress in our homes. This acronym is called the PERMA Model:

Seligman's PERMA Model[61]

P: Positive Emotion: "It is the ability to remain optimistic and view one's past, present, and future from a constructive perspective."
(www.positivepsychology.com)

E: Engagement: "Activities that meet our need for engagement flood the body with positive neurctransmitters and hormones that elevate one's sense of well-being. This engagement helps us remain present, as well as synthesize the activities where we find calm, focus, and joy."
(www.positivepsychology.com)

---

[61]   https://positivepsychology.com/perma-model/

R: Relationships: "Positive relationships with one's parents, siblings, peers, coworkers, and friends is a key ingredient to overall joy. Strong relationships also provide support in difficult times that require resilience."
(www.positivepsychology.com)

M: Meaning: "Religion and spirituality provide many people with meaning, as can working for a good company, raising children, volunteering for a greater cause, and expressing ourselves creatively."
(www.positivepsychology.com)

A: Accomplishments: "Having goals and ambition in life can help us to achieve things that can give us a sense of accomplishment. You should make realistic goals that can be met, and just putting in the effort to achieving those goals can already give you a sense of satisfaction. When you finally achieve those goals, a sense of pride and fulfillment will be reached."
(www.postivepyschology.com)

Breaking the Cyber Code
Part 2

National Initiative for Cybersecurity Education (NICE) Cybersecurity Workforce Framework[62]

This publication describes the National Initiative for Cybersecurity Education (NICE) Cybersecurity Workforce Framework (NICE Framework), a reference structure that describes the interdisciplinary nature of the cybersecurity work. It serves as a fundamental reference and resource for describing and sharing information about cybersecurity work and the knowledge, skills, and abilities (KSAs) needed to complete tasks that can strengthen the cybersecurity posture of an organization. It is a common, consistent lexicon that categorizes and describes cybersecurity work. In addition, the NICE Framework improves the communication of how to identify, recruit, develop, and retain cybersecurity talent.

In this Breaking The Cyber Code Series, I will reference the fifty-two different information technology work roles, which are the most detailed groupings of cybersecurity and related work which also include a list of attributes required to perform that role in the form of knowledge, skills, and abilities (KSAs), and tasks performed in that role.

1st NICE Framework IT Role

Job Title: *All Source-Collection Manager*

This role identifies collection authorities and environment; incorporates priority information requirements into collection management; develops concepts to meet leadership's intent. Determines capabilities of available collection assets, identifies new collection capabilities;

---

62   National Institute of Standards and Technology Special Publication 800-181.
https://csrc.nist.gov/publications/detail/sp/800-181/final

and constructs and disseminates collection plans. In addition, this role monitors execution of tasked collection to ensure effective execution of the collection plan.

The NICE Framework describes abilities as the competence to perform an observable behavior or a behavior that results in an observable product.

IT Role Abilities:

- Ability to apply collaborative skills and strategies.

- Ability to apply critical reading/thinking skills.

- Ability to coordinate and collaborate with analysts regarding surveillance requirements and essential information development.

- Ability to coordinate, collaborate, and disseminate information to subordinate, lateral, and higher-level organizations.

- Ability to correctly employ each organization or element into the collection plan and matrix.

Category: Collect and Operate

Specialty Area: Collection Operations

Suggested Education: Bachelor of Arts or Bachelor of Science Degree

Funding Resources for Training: Governor's Talent Investment Agency-Workforce Development and Local Workforce Development Fund

Types of Industry Certifications: CompTIA A+, CompTIA Network +, CompTIA Security +, Certified Business Intelligence Professional, Certified Software Business Analyst

Possible U.S. Salary Ranges: $36,000-62,000+

Similar U.S. Industry Job Titles: Operations Manager, Intelligence Manager

Summary

As you can see there are tech jobs out there today that pay a good salary with minimal requirements if you have the will and the know-how. The resources are out there ready for you to obtain them, so let me coach you on this.

Coaching Time

Ask yourself these powerful coaching questions:

1. What do I need right now?

2. What opportunity does this challenge present?

3. What is stopping me from taking the next steps to achieve a worthwhile STEM career that has sustainability and job security for the foreseeable future?

Quote of the Day

"Your level of success is determined by your level of discipline and perseverance."

~ Author Unknown

National Initiative for Cybersecurity Education (NICE) Cybersecurity Workforce Framework

2nd NICE Framework IT Role

Job Title: Collection Requirements Manager

Evaluate collection operations and develop effects-based collection requirements strategies using available sources and methods to improve collection. Develop, process, validate, and coordinate submission of collection requirements. Evaluate performance of collection assets and collection operations.

IT Role Abilities

- Ability to apply collaborative skills and strategies.
- Ability to apply critical reading/thinking skills.
- Ability to coordinate, collaborate, and disseminate information to subordinate, lateral, and higher-level organizations.

Category: Collect and Operate

Specialty Area: Collection Operations

Similar U.S. Industry Titles: Information Security Analyst, Senior Manager Advance Analytics

Suggested Education: Bachelor's degree required. Degree in Cybersecurity or Computer Science preferred.

Types of Industry Certifications: CompTIA Security +, Certified Ethical Hacker, Certified Computing Professional, Certified Forensic Computer Examiner, Professional Cloud Security Manager Certification, Licensed Penetration Tester, GIAC Certified Intrusion Analyst

Funding for Training: U.S. Small Business Administration and employer-funded reimbursements.

U.S. Salary Ranges: $56,000-153,000+

Summary

As you can see, as we advance in the NICE Cybersecurity Framework job titles, you will require more education, knowledge, and skills in order to be ready and prepared for this type of role. The salary does vary. based on the amount of experience you have and the type of industry and the size of the business the person is working in, such as a healthcare organization or a financial institution, to name a few.

Be prepared to think on your feet and analyze numerous amounts of data points from various applications, databases, end points, and other information resources to provide a comprehensive summary report of your findings to inform your organization and other staff members. This will help your leaders make better critical decisions on how to protect its valuable assets.

Coaching Time

Ask yourself these powerful coaching questions:

1.   What's really holding me back?

2.   What can I do *right now* to get one step closer to my goal?

3.   What will I gain by reaching this goal?

Quote of the Day

"It's not about the goal. It's about becoming the type of person that can accomplish the goal."

~ Author Unknown

National Initiative for Cybersecurity Education (NICE) Cybersecurity Workforce Framework

3rd NICE Framework IT Role

Job Tile: Source Analyst

Analyze data/information from one or multiple sources to conduct preparation of the environment, respond to requests for information, and submit intelligence collection and production requirements in support of planning and operations.

Category: Analyze

Specialty Area: All-Source Analysis

IT Role Abilities:

- Ability to communicate complex information, concepts, or ideas in a confident and well-organized manner through verbal, written, and/or visual means.

- Ability to accurately and completely source all data used in intelligence, assessment and/or planning products.

- Ability to clearly articulate intelligence requirements into well-formulated research questions and data tracking variables for inquiry tracking purposes.

- Ability to develop or recommend analytic approaches or solutions to problems and situations for which information is incomplete or for which no precedent exists.

- Ability to effectively collaborate via virtual teams.

- Ability to evaluate information for reliability, validity, and relevance.

- Ability to evaluate, analyze, and synthesize large quantities of data (which may be fragmented and contradictory) into high-quality, fused targeting/intelligence products.

- Ability to exercise judgment when policies are not well-defined.
- Ability to focus research efforts to meet the customer's decision-making needs.
- Ability to function effectively in a dynamic, fast-paced environment.
- Ability to function in a collaborative environment, seeking continuous consultation with other analysts and experts—both internal and external to the organization—to leverage analytical and technical expertise.
- Ability to identify intelligence gaps.
- Ability to recognize and mitigate cognitive biases which may affect analysis.
- Ability to recognize and mitigate deception in reporting and analysis.
- Ability to think critically.
- Ability to think like threat actors.
- Ability to understand objectives and effects.
- Ability to utilize multiple intelligence sources across all intelligence disciplines.

Similar U.S. Industry Titles: Operations Analyst, Data Analyst, Cybersecurity Analyst

Suggested Education/Work Experience: Bachelor's degree and/or 5+ years of professional IT experience and 2+ years of information security experience.

Types of Industry Certifications: GIAC Certified Intrusion Analyst, Information Security Analyst, GIAC Certified Firewall Analyst, EC-Council Certified Security Analyst, CompTIA Network+, CompTIA Security+, Associate of International Information Systems Security Certification Consortium, Certified Information System Security Professional

Funding for Training (Grants may be available such as these): Community College Cyber Pilot (C3P) Program; Advanced Technological Education (ATE); Training-Based Workforce Development for Advanced Cyberinfrastructure (CyberTraining); Secure and Trustworthy Cyberspace (SaTC)

U.S. Salary Ranges: $37,000-$63,000+

Summary

As you can see, there is a lot of data analysis in this IT role. The data points will be coming from many sources, and you will need to be able to consolidate and report on the relevant findings. Remember to think like a threat actor when it comes to reporting on the possible risks so you can help your organization better protect itself from bad actors and the possible threats. Be sure to report on all the necessary critical information needed so stakeholders can make an educated decision on how to act on those findings.

Coaching Time

Ask yourself these powerful coaching questions:

1. Am I ready to do whatever it takes to reach my goals?

2. What opportunity does this challenge present?

3. What do I need right now?

Quote of the Day

"There will always be someone who can't see your worth. Don't le⁻ it be you!"

~ Author Unknown

National Initiative for Cybersecurity Education (NICE) Cybersecurity Workforce Framework

4th NICE Framework IT Role

Job Tile: Authorizing Official/Designating Representative

Senior official or executive with the authority to formally assume responsibility for operating an information system at an acceptable level of risk to organizational operations (including mission, functions, image, or reputation), organizational assets, individuals, other organizations, and the nation (CNSSI 4009).

Category: Securely Provision

Specialty Area: Risk Management

IT Role Abilities:

- Ability to assess and forecast manpower requirements to meet organizational objectives.

- Ability to develop policy, plans, and strategy in compliance with laws, regulations, policies, and standards in support of organizational cyber activities.

- Ability to coordinate cyber operations with other organization functions or support activities.

- Ability to identify external partners with common cyber operations interests.

- Ability to interpret and apply laws, regulations, policies, and guidance relevant to organization cyber objectives.

- Ability to work across departments and business units to implement the organization's privacy principles and programs, and align privacy objectives with security objectives.

- Abi ity to relate strategy, business, and technology in the context of organizational dynamics.

- Ability to understand technology, management, and leadership issues related to organization processes anc problem solving.

- Abil ty to understand the basic concepts and issues related to cyber and its organizational impact.

- Ability to apply cybersecurity and privacy principles to organizational requirements (relevant to con¬identiality, integrity, availability, authentication, and non-repudiation).

- Abili¬y to identify critical infrastructure systems with information communication technology that were designed without system security considerations.

Similar U.S. Industry Titles: Associate Vice President/Deputy Chief Information Officer, Director, Privacy and Information Security Risk and Governance, Deputy Information Privacy Officer, Deputy Information Security Officer

Suggested Education/Work Experience: Bachelor's Degree and 8 years large-scale enterprise IT management experience of which 5 years of demonstrated leadership experience has been in the management of an Information Security Department with oversight over all information security disciplines.

Types of Industry Certifications: Certified Information Privacy Professional, GIAC Security Leadership Certification, Certified Information Privacy Technologist, Associate of International Information Systems Security Certification Consortium, Certified Information System Security Professional, System Security Certified

Practitioner, Certified Information Privacy Manager, Certified Information Security Manager

Funding for Training (Private foundations may have grants available such as these): Lumina Foundation, MacArthur Foundation, Bill & Melinda Gates Foundation Postsecondary Success

U.S. Salary Ranges: $118,000-$167,000+

Summary

As you can see, this IT role demands a lot of leadership responsibilities and requires several years of information technology experience and management experience across different information security disciplines. This leader will focus on aligning strategy and technology to business goals which will be a necessary skill set.

Be prepared to communicate your strategic plans across the organization including to external bodies in order to gain support for the vision and cooperation from all stakeholders involved.

Coaching Time

Ask yourself these powerful coaching questions:

1. What is critical here for me?

2. What am I sacrificing by staying where I am?

3. Do I want help with this?

Quote of the Day

"The best and most beautiful things in the world cannot be seen or even touched—they must be felt with the heart."

~ Helen Keller

National Initiative for Cybersecurity Education (NICE) Cybersecurity Workforce Framework

5th NICE Framework IT Role

Job Tile: Communications Security (COMSEC) Manager

Manage the Communications Security (COMSEC) resources of an organization (CNSSI 4009) or key custodian for a Crypto Key Management System (CKMS).

Category: Oversee and Govern

Specialty Area: Cybersecurity Management

IT Role Abilities:

- Ability to recognize the unique aspects of the Communications Security (COMSEC) environment and hierarchy.

- Ability to interpret Communications Security (COMSEC) terminology, guidelines, and procedures.

- Ability to identify the roles and responsibilities for appointed Communications Security (COMSEC) personnel.

- Ability to manage Communications Security (COMSEC) material accounting, control, and use procedure.

- Ability to identify types of Communications Security (COMSEC) incidents and how they are reported.

- Ability to recognize the importance of auditing Communications Security (COMSEC) material and accounts.

- Ability to Identify the requirements of in-process accounting for Communications Security (COMSEC).

Similar U.S. Industry Titles: Security Management Specialist, Information Security Analyst, Computer and Information Systems Manager, Information Security Manager, Information Systems Assurance Manager

Suggested Education/Work Experience: Bachelor's degree in Computer Science or Information Systems required and 5 to 10 years of IT experience (preferably 3+ years of information security experience).

Types of Industry Certifications: GIAC Certified Project Manager, GIAC Security Leadership Certification, EC-Council Chief Information Security Officer, CompTIA Advanced Security Practitioner, Computer Network Architects, Certified Information Security Manager, Certified Information System Security Professional

Funding for Training (Federal government initiatives may be available such as these): Cybercareers.gov; Federal Cyber Reskilling Academy; Presidential Management Fellows Program; Cyber Corps Scholarship Services; Cybersecurity Talent Initiative

U.S. Salary Ranges: $56,000-153,000+

Summary

This role is focused mainly on communication security and how data is transferred securely on all devices to ensure the confidentiality, integrity, and nonrepudiation of the information in transit or at rest. Be familiar with the seven layers of the Open Systems Interconnection (OSI) model of computer networking and how data encryption processing works. Also, be knowledgeable of information system auditing, verification, and how to ensure that there is proper information logging in place.

Coaching Time

Ask yourself these powerful coaching questions:

1. What do I want, how bad do I want it, and what am I willing to do to get it?

2. What conversation is it time to have?

3. What outcome do I want?

Quote of the Day

"Not all storms come to disrupt your life; some come to clear your path."

~ Author unknown

National Initiative for Cybersecurity Education (NICE) Cybersecurity Workforce Framework

6th NICE Framework IT Role

Job Title: Cyber Crime Investigator

Identify, collect, examine, and preserve evidence using controlled and documented analytical and investigative techniques.

Category: Investigate

Specialty Area: Cyber Investigation

IT Role Abilities:

- Ability to find and navigate the dark web using the TOR network to locate markets and forums.

- Ability to examine digital media on multiple operating system platforms.

Similar U.S. Industry Titles: Forensic Science Technician, Information Security Analysts, Incident Response Lead, Information Security Team Lead

Types of Industry Certifications: Certified Computer Crime Investigator, The Certified Information Privacy Professional, Certified Forensic Interviewer, Licensed Penetration Tester, GIAC Certified Forensics Analyst

Suggested Education/Work Experience: Minimum 7 years of experience in Information Security and Engineering roles of increasing responsibility, resulting in strong familiarity with application and network security.

Funding for training/education (Scholarships may be available such as these): AECT McJulien Graduate Student Scholarship Award; Arlyn Scales Award for Science and Technology; Eli Lilly and Company BDPA Scholarship; Innovation in Sales Technology Scholarship

U.S. Salary Ranges: $53,000-162,000+

Coaching Time:

Ask yourself these powerful coaching questions:

1.   What is here that I want to explore?

2.   Whct kind of plan do I need to create?

3.   If I could do it over again, what would I do differently?

Quote of the Day:

"The bes⁻ way to predict your future is to create it."

~ *Abraham Lincoln*

National Initiative for Cybersecurity Education (NICE) Cybersecurity Workforce Framework

7th NICE Framework IT Role

Job Tile: Cyber Defense Analyst

Use data collected from a variety of cyber defense tools (e.g., IDS alerts, firewalls, network traffic logs) to analyze events that occur within their environments for the purposes of mitigating threats.

Category: Protect and Defend

Specialty Area: Cyber Defense Analysis

IT Role Abilities:

- Ability to analyze malware.

- Ability to conduct vulnerability scans and recognize vulnerabilities in security systems.

- Ability to accurately and completely source all data used in intelligence, assessment, and/or planning products.

- Ability to apply cybersecurity and privacy principles to organizational requirements (relevant to confidentiality, integrity, availability, authentication, non-repudiation).

- Ability to apply techniques for detecting host and network-based intrusions using intrusion detection technologies.

- Ability to interpret the information collected by network tools (e.g. Nslookup, Ping, and Traceroute).

Similar U.S. Industry Titles: Cyber Security Analyst, Cyber Counterintelligence Analyst, Information Security Analysts, Computer Systems Analysts, Computer Network Support Specialists

Types of Industry Certifications: GIAC Certified Firewall Analyst, GIAC Certified Intrusion Analyst, CompTIA Network+, CompTIA Security+, Information System Analyst, Certified Cyber Forensics Professional

Suggested Education/Work Experience: 1+ years of experience within the Info Sec industry or comparable technical troubleshooting, networking, or security experiences. Be coachable and inclined to continuous improvement.

Funding for Training/Education (Scholarships may be available as referenced by the International Consortium of Minority Cybersecurity Professionals (ICMCP) website): ICMCP-Security Innovation Cyber-Ready Certification; The Marci McCarthy Cybersecurity Certification Scholarship Program; Aric K. Perminter Endowment Fellowship; The Lynx Technology Partners Scholarship; The Nelson H. Waits, Sr. Education Fund; Yeshiva University-Graduate Dean's Scholarship in Cybersecurity

U.S. Salary Ranges: $29,000-$185,000+

Summary

As you can see, in the Information Technology industry, you will need to be mentally sharp and take good care of your mind and body in order to be your best self. This role will require a lot of analytical work and you may even have long days and nights just to be able to defend against bad actors who are attacking twenty-four hours/seven days a week. The role will be exciting and challenging at the same time, but every day will be different, and that is what is so gratifying about it.

Coaching Time:

Ask yourself these powerful coaching questions:

1.　What resources are available to me?

2.　When will I act on them?

3.　Now what?

Quote of the Day:

"Don't wish for it, work for it."

~ Author Unknown

National Initiative for Cybersecurity Education (NICE) Cybersecurity Workforce Framework

8th NICE Framework IT Role

Job Tile: Cyber Defense Forensics Analyst

Analyze digital evidence and investigate computer security incidents to derive useful information in support of system/network vulnerability mitigation.

Category: Investigate

Specialty Area: Digital Forensics

IT Role Abilities:

- Ability to decrypt digital data collections.
- Ability to conduct forensic analyses in and for both Windows and Unix/Linux environments.

Similar U.S. Industry Titles: Cyber Threat Analysts, Security Operations Analysts, Security Management Specialists, Information Security Analysts

Types of Industry Certifications: Certified Cyber Forensics Professional, GIAC Certified Forensics Analyst, Information System Analyst

Suggested Education/Work Experience: Bachelor's degree in an applicable field such cs Information Assurance/Computer Science or equivalent industry experience, and 2+ years of professional experience in the field of cybersecurity.

Funding for Training/Education (Scholarships may be available such as these): Quality Company Formations Scholarship, R&D Systems Scholarship Program, Spokeo Connections Scholarship, The America Life Fund Scholarship, The Sure Oak Scholarship

U.S. Salary Ranges: $43,000-$114,000+

Summary

As you can see this IT role will require the use of decryption tools and forensics analysts methods to conduct cyber investigations which may require an array of different discovery products that would help law enforcement and other external parties get the data they need and determine the chain of custody details to report on cyber-attacks. Become familiar with most operating systems and industry software tools in the market so you can have the expertise needed to assist any organization's cyber investigation.

Coaching Time

Ask yourself these powerful coaching questions:

1. What is my powerful why?

2. What do I long for?

3. What do I like to do that makes me come alive?

Quote of the Day

"Being happy doesn't mean everything is perfect; it means you've decided to see beyond the imperfections."

~ Gerard Way

National Initiative for Cybersecurity Education (NICE) Cybersecurity Workforce Framework

9th NICE Framework IT Role

Job Title: Cyber Defense Incident Responder

Investigate, analyze, and respond to cyber incidents within the network environment or enclave.

Category: Protect and Defend

Specialty Area: Incident Response

IT Role Abilities:

- Ability to design incident response for cloud service models.

- Ability to apply techniques for detecting host and network-based intrusions using intrusion detection technologies.

Suggested Education/Work Experience: Bachelor's degree in related field or equivalent work experience.

Funding Resources for Training: (Scholarships may be available such as these): AECT Foundation Mentor Endowment Scholarship, Bluepay STEM Scholarship, Boomer Benefits Scholarship, Clubs of America, Courage to Grow Scholarships

Types of Industry Certifications: CSX Expert, Certified Cyber Forensics Professional, GIAC Certified Incident Handler, Certified Network Defense Architect, CompTIA Security+, GIAC Certified Forensics Analysts, GIAC Certified Firewall Analysts

Possible U.S. Salary Ranges: $75,000-$150,500+

Similar U.S. Industry Job Titles: Cyber Incident Response Analysts, Security Incident Response Engineer, Information Security Analysts, Security Operations and Cyber Incident Response Lead, Cyber Security Threat Analysts, Cyber Security Engineer

Summary

As you can see, this IT role has minimum requirements. You may be able to obtain this job opportunity by gaining the equivalent of a four-year degree, on-the-job training, or the related work experience. Prepare to continuously learn in different work environments and industries, which will increase your marketability. In addition, try to obtain the necessary industry IT certifications to increase your skill set and advance your knowledge base for future roles which may be of interest to you throughout your cybersecurity career.

Coaching Time

Ask yourself these powerful coaching questions:

1. What do I believe is the first step?

2. What if it doesn't happen?

3. What is the risk?

Quote of the Day

"You will face many defeats in your life, but never let yourself be defeated."

~ Maya Angelou

National Initiative for Cybersecurity Education (NICE) Cybersecurity Workforce Framework

10th NICE Framework IT Role

Job Title: Cyber Defense Infrastructure Support Specialist

Test, implement, deploy, maintain, and administer the infrastructure hardware and software.

Category: Protect and Defend

Specialty Area: Cyber Defense Infrastructure Support

IT Role Abilities:

- Ability to apply cybersecurity and privacy principles to organizational requirements (relevant to confidentiality, integrity, availability, authentication, non-repudiation).

Suggested Education/Work Experience: Bachelor's degree in Information Systems, Computer Science, or equivalent work experience in the requested field.

Funding Resources for Training (Scholarships may be available such as these): HostGator Website Scholarship, Instructional Design & Learning Technologies Scholarship, John Glaser Scholarship, MIE Solutions Scholarship Opportunity

Types of Industry Certifications: CompTIA Network+, Certified Wireless Specialist, Certified Network Defense Architect, Certified Wireless Technology Specialist, Global Industrial Cyber Security Specialist, CompTIA Security+

Similar U.S. Industry Job Titles: Solution Architect, Computer Network Support Specialists, Security Management Specialists, IT Enterprise Architect, Cyber

Security Analysts, Cyber Infrastructure Engineer, Cyber Defense Analysts

Possible U.S. Salary Ranges: $12,182-$80,082+

Summary

As you may have determined, this IT Role has minimal requirements and pays a wide range in compensation. Your income level will be based on your work experience, education, and the IT certifications you may possess at the time of applying for that role. Stay on top of industry trends and continuing education units because that will determine your career trajectory in the foreseeable future.

Coaching Time

Ask yourself these powerful coaching questions:

1. If my life depended on taking action, what would I do?

2. What could I plan to do about it?

3. How do I suppose it will all work out?

Quote of the Day

"Go confidently in the directions of your dream! Live the life you've imagined."

~ Henry David Thoreau

National Initiative for Cybersecurity Education (NICE) Cybersecurity Workforce Framework

11th NICE Framework IT Role

Job Title: Cyber Instructional Curriculum Developer

Develop, plan, coordinate, and evaluate cyber training/education courses, methods, and techniques based on instructional needs.

Category: Oversee and Govern

Specialty Area: Training, Education, and Awareness

IT Role Abilities:

- Ability to develop curriculum that speaks to the topic at the appropriate level for the target audience.

- Ability to communicate complex information, concepts, or ideas in a confident and well-organized manner through verbal, written, and/or visual means.

- Ability to conduct vulnerability scans and recognize vulnerabilities in security systems.

- Ability to prepare and present briefings.

- Ability to produce technical documentation.

- Ability to apply principles of adult learning.

- Ability to develop clear directions and instructional materials.

- Ability to develop curriculum for use within a virtual environment.

- Ability to apply the Instructional System Design (ISD) methodology.

- Ability to operate common network tools (e.g., ping, traceroute, nslookup).

- Ability to tailor curriculum that speaks to the topic at the appropriate level for the target audience.

- Ability to execute OS command line (e.g., ipconfig, netstat, dir, nbtstat).

- Ability to operate different electronic communication systems and methods (e.g., email, VOIP, IM, web forums, Direct Video Broadcasts).

- Ability to apply critical reading/thinking skills.

- Ability to evaluate information for reliability, validity, and relevance.

- Ability to function in a collaborative environment, seeking continuous consultation with other analysts and experts—both internal and external to the organization—to leverage analytical and technical expertise.

- Ability to tailor technical and planning information to a customer's level of understanding.

- Ability to think critically.

- Ability to monitor advancements in information privacy technologies to ensure organizational adaptation and compliance.

- Ability to develop or procure curriculum that speaks to the topic at the appropriate level for the target.

- Ability to understand technology, management, and leadership issues related to organization processes and problem solving.

- Ability to understand the basic concepts and issues related to cyber and its organizational impact.

- Ability to conduct training and education needs assessment.

Suggested Education/Work Experience: Preferred degrees include Computer Science, Computer Engineering, Electrical Engineering, Information Technology, Information Systems, or an equivalent degree. Must have at least 5 years of experience in and knowledge of operating system and network security.

Funding Resources for Training (Scholarships may be available such as these): Professional Woman's Magazine Scholarship Opportunity, Red Olive Women in STEM Scholarship, Vison Tech Camps Scholarship, After College STEM Inclusion Scholarship

Types of Industry Certifications: Global Industrial Cyber Security Professional, Certified Cyber Security Professional, Certified Information System Security Professional, Information Systems Analyst, Certified Employment Support Professional

Possible U.S. Salary Ranges: $62,300-$98,000+

Similar U.S. Industry Job Titles: Information Systems and Technology Faculty Member, Technical Instructor, Technical Course Developer, Information Security Instructor, Corporate Trainer, Cyber Instructor and Curriculum Developer, Curriculum Manager, Cyber Security Subject Matter Expert, Instructional Developer

Summary

As you can very well see, this IT role requires you to be well-versed in the knowledge and skills of cybersecurity, and you will need to:

- Be able to communicate effectively about your expertise in the tools and industry experiences.

- Be familiar with the way people learn as visual learners, lecture-style learners, and reading and writing communication learners.

- Be interesting, engaging, and flexible with your methods of teaching.

Coaching Time

Ask yourself these powerful coaching questions:

1. What outcome do I want?

2. How does this fit with my plans, way of life, or my values?

3. What do I have to do to get the job done?

Quote of the Day

"A goal without a plan is just a wish."

~ Antoine de Saint-Exupéry

National Initiative for Cybersecurity Education (NICE) Cybersecurity Workforce Framework

12th NICE Framework IT Role

Job Title: Cyber Instructor

Develop and conduct training or education of personnel within the cyber domain.

Category: Oversee and Govern

Specialty Area: Training, Education, and Awareness

IT Role Abilities:

- Ability to prepare and deliver education and awareness briefings to ensure that systems, network, and data users are aware of and adhere to systems security policies and procedures.

- Ability to answer questions in a clear and concise manner.

- Ability to ask clarifying questions.

- Ability to communicate complex information, concepts, or ideas in a confident and well-organized manner through verbal, written, and/or visual means.

- Ability to communicate effectively when writing.

- Ability to conduct vulnerability scans and recognize vulnerabilities in security systems.

- Ability to facilitate small group discussions.

- Ability to gauge learner understanding and knowledge level.

- Ability to prepare and present briefings.

- Ability to produce technical documentation.

- Ability to provide effective feedback to students for improving learning.

- Ability to apply principles of adult learning.

- Ability to design valid and reliable assessments.

- Ability to develop clear directions and instructional materials.

- Ability to develop curriculum for use within a virtual environment.

- Ability to leverage best practices and lessons learned of external organizations and academic institutions dealing with cyber issues.

- Ability to operate common network tools (e.g., ping, traceroute, nslookup).

- Ability to tailor curriculum that speaks to the topic at the appropriate level for the target audience.

- Ability to execute OS command line (e.g., ipconfig, netstat, dir, nbtstat).

- Ability to operate different electronic communication systems and methods (e.g., email, VOIP, IM, web forums, Direct Video Broadcasts).

- Ability to accurately and completely source all data used in intelligence, assessment, and/or planning products.

- Ability to apply critical reading/thinking skills.

- Ability to evaluate information for reliability, validity, and relevance.

- Ability to function in a collaborative environment, seeking continuous consultation with other analysts and experts—both internal and external to the organization—to leverage analytical and technical expertise.

- Ab lity to tailor technical and planning information to a customer's level of understanding.

- Ab lity to think critically.

- Ab lity to monitor advancements in information privacy technologies to ensure organizational adaptation and compliance.

- Ability to develop or procure curriculum that speaks to the topic at the appropriate level for the target.

- Ability to understand technology, management, and leadership issues related to organizational processes and problem solving.

- Ability to understand the basic concepts and issues related to cyber and its organizational impact.

- Ability to conduct training and education needs assessment.

Suggested Education/Work Experience: Associate degree or higher and 3+ years in-field occupational experience with relevant networking, operating system, and security certifications.

Funding Resources for Training (Scholarships may be available such as these): Facebook Fellowship Program, Gear Upz Your Future, AAUW American Fellowship, ASIS Foundation Chapter Matching Scholarship, EAPSI Fellowships

Types of Industry Certifications: Certified Cyber Forensics Professional, Certified Professional Instructor, Certified EC-Council Instructor, Global Industrial Cyber Security Professional, Certified Cyber Security Professional, Certified Wireless Network Trainer, CSX Expert, Certified Information System Security Professional

Possible U.S. Salary Ranges: $64,500-$114,000+

Similar U.S. Industry Job Titles: Adjunct Instructor-Cyber Security, IT/Network Security Instructor, Senior Training Specialist, Online-Adjunct Instructor-Computer Information Systems, Cyber Security Apprentice Instructor, Cyber/IT Instructor

Summary

As you can see, this IT role has several requirements related to critical thinking, knowing adult learning styles, and it states you will need to have familiarity with how to develop instructional and visual aid material for the cyber curriculum and corresponding course. A minimum of an associate degree may be required in some cases when teaching in K-12 or at a community college. When teaching at universities or other 4-year colleges, a more advanced degree of education will be required. Try to stay abreast of the latest cyber security threats and cyber-related news stories and new terminology in the field, including software products, so you will be able to provide relevant details to your students in real-time of current events.

Coaching Time

Ask yourself these powerful coaching questions:

1. What is the single, most meaningful change I can make in this area?

2. If I could not fail, what would the goal be?

3. How can I raise the bar and embrace a higher standard?

Quote of the Day

"Create the life you can't wait to wake up to."

~ *Jen Coleman*

National Initiative for Cybersecurity Education (NICE) Cybersecurity Workforce Framework

13th NICE Framework IT Role

Job Title: Cyber Intel Planner

Develop detailed intelligence plans to satisfy cyber operations requirements. Collaborate with cyber operations planners to identify, validate, and levy requirements for collection and analysis. Participate in targeting selection, validation, synchronization, and execution of cyber actions. Synchronize intelligence activities to support organization objectives in cyberspace.

Category: Collect and Operate

Specialty Area: Cyber Operational Planning

IT Role Abilities:

◆ Ability to communicate complex information, concepts, or ideas in a confident and well-organized manner through verbal, written, and/or visual means.

• Ability to accurately and completely source all data used in intelligence, assessment, and/or planning products.

• Ability to adjust to and operate in a diverse, unpredictable, challenging, and fast-paced work environment.

• Ability to apply approved planning, development, and staffing processes.

• Ability to apply critical reading/thinking skills.

• Ability to collaborate effectively with others.

- Ability to coordinate cyber operations with other organization functions or support activities.

- Ability to develop or recommend planning solutions to problems and situations for which no precedent exists.

- Ability to effectively collaborate via virtual teams.

- Ability to exercise judgment when policies are not well-defined.

- Ability to function in a collaborative environment, seeking continuous consultation with other analysts and experts—both internal and external to the organization—to leverage analytical and technical expertise.

- Ability to identify external partners with common cyber operations interests.

- Ability to interpret and apply laws, regulations, policies, and guidance relevant to organization cyber objectives.

- Ability to interpret and understand complex and rapidly-evolving concepts.

- Ability to participate as a member of planning teams, coordination groups, and task forces as necessary.

- Ability to tailor technical and planning information to a customer's level of understanding.

- Ability to translate, track, and prioritize information needs and intelligence collection requirements across the extended enterprise.

Suggested Education/Work Experience: High school diploma and 11 to 14 years of experience, or Bachelor of Arts /Bachelor of Science degree and 5 to 10 years of experience, or Master of Arts/Master of Science and 3 to 6 years of experience.

Funding Resources for Training: (Scholarships may be available such as these): Google US/Canada PhD Fellowship, Influenster Code Like a Girl Scholarship, MSGC Undergraduate Under-Represented Minority Fellowship Program, NDSGC American Indian Scholarships, Trendhim Scholarship, 10X Digital Marketing Scholarship

Types of Industry Certifications: Certified Ethical Hacker, Certified Cyber Forensics Professional, Intelligence Planner Certification Program, Global Industrial Cyber Security Professional, Certified Cyber Security Professional, Certified Network Defender, CSX Expert, Certified Information System Security Professional, Security Clearance may be required.

Possible U.S. Salary Ranges: $41,500-$162,500+

Similar U.S. Industry Job Titles: Cyber Intelligence Analyst, Cyber Target Analyst, Mission Command-Computer Information Systems, Cyber Fires Analyst, Senior Information Security Engineer, Intel Tradecraft Developer/Trainer, Intelligence Program Manager, Cyberspace Analyst, Weapons and Tactics Analyst

Summary

This IT role is very intriguing and may require a government security clearance because of the sensitive classified nature of the intelligence information. You will need to analyze numerous data points and other significant details, so be prepared to use your critical-thinking skills consistently in order to meet the needs of internal and external team member requests. Be familiar with U.S. and international laws and treaties because information will be coming from a vast array of sources. Keep abreast of new federal, state, and local regulations, laws, standards, guidance, and policies which may influence your work.

Coaching Time

Ask yourself these powerful coaching questions:

1.   What message is being offered in this situation?

2.   What do I want to be different in my life one year from now?

3.   How do I want to celebrate my milestones?

Quote of the Day

"The greatest pleasure in life is doing what people say you can't do."

~ Walter Bagehot

National Initiative for Cybersecurity Education (NICE) Cybersecurity Workforce Framework

14th NICE Framework IT Role

Job Title: Cyber Legal Advisor

Provide legal advice and recommendations on relevant topics related to cyber law.

Category: Oversee and Govern

Specialty Area: Legal Advice and Advocacy

IT Role Abilities:

- Ability to monitor and assess the potential impact of emerging technologies on laws, regulations, and/or policies.

Suggested Education/Work Experience: Bachelor of Arts or Bachelor of Science degree and 8+ years of experience as an all-source intelligence analyst and 5+ years of experience writing analytic reports or papers.

Funding Resources for Training (Scholarships may be available such as these): Ford Foundation Diversity Fellowships, Full Stack Student Scholarship, Girls in STEM (GIS) Scholarship, Global Entrepreneur's Award, Maley/FTE Scholarship

Types of Industry Certifications: Accredited Legal Professional, Certified Cyber Forensics Professional, Certified Information System Security Professional, Certified Legal Investigator, Global Industrial Cyber Security Professional, Certified Cyber Security Professional, Certified Information Security Manager, GIAC Certified Forensics Examiner

Possible U.S. Salary Ranges: $21,500-170,000+

Similar U.S. Industry Job Titles: Lead Cyber Threat Analyst, Cyber Security Analyst, Chief Information Security Officer, Chief Information Officer, Cybersecurity Awareness Advisor, Cybersecurity Subject Matter Expert (SME), Cyber Watch Analyst

Summary

As you can see, in this IT role, your cybersecurity expertise and knowledge of all types of technology and cyber threats will be necessary to effectively provide the proper analysis to your individual stakeholders so they know the potential risks when building, implementing, and maintaining secure infrastructure and information systems. Intelligence briefing reporting may be required on an ongoing basis to keep everyone aware of changes in the threat landscape and new policies, laws, regulations, and industry standards. Be sure to subscribe to relevant information and new sources to keep abreast of new threats.

Coaching Time

Ask yourself these powerful coaching questions:

1. What is the low-lying fruit it is time for me to take advantage of?

2. What goal would really get me excited?

3. What have I always wished I could accomplish?

Quote of the Day

"There is no passion to be found playing small—in settling for a life that is less than the one you are capable of living."

~ *Nelson Mandela*

National Initiative for Cybersecurity Education (NICE) Cybersecurity Workforce Framework

15th NICE Framework IT Role

Job Title: Cyber Operator 1

Conduct collection, processing, and/or geolocation of systems to exploit, locate, and/or track targets of interest. Perform network navigation, tactical forensic analysis, and, when directed, execute on-net operations.

Category: Collect and Operate

Specialty Area: Cyber Operations

IT Role Abilities:

- Ability to interpret and translate customer requirements into operational action.
- Ability to monitor system operations and react to events in response to triggers and/or observation of trends or unusual activity.
- Ability to perform network collection tactics, techniques, and procedures to include decryption capabilities/tools.
- Ability to perform wireless collection procedures to include decryption capabilities/tools.

Suggested Education/Work Experience: Bachelor's degree or equivalent, and 2+ years of relevant experience; strong network troubleshooting skills (especially Layer 2 and Layer 3).

Funding Resources for Training (Scholarships may be available such as these): National Debt Relief Scholarship, Technology-Students Scholarship Program, The Sweet Flow Digital Marketing Scholarship, Websauce Web Design Scholarship

Types of Industry Certifications: Certified Cyber Forensics Professional, CompTIA Network+, CompTIA Security+, Certified Cyber Security Professional, Certified Network Defender, CSX Expert

Possible U.S. Salary Ranges: $27,000-$75,000+

Similar U.S. Industry Job Titles: Network Operations Specialist, Cyber Defense Operator, Network Security Technician, Cyber Security Engineer, Information Security Operator, Cyber Security Analyst, Systems Engineer, Cyber Network Professional

Summary

As you can see, this IT role is a great way to start your cybersecurity career on the ground floor and have a lot of growth potential and advancement opportunities in other areas of the field. Employers may hire you with the equivalent work history of a college degree and you may be able to obtain this role with the experience you already possess. Make sure to at least get some industry certifications so you increase your chances of landing the job.

Coaching Time[63]

Ask yourself these powerful coaching questions:

1. What do I want to learn, and how do I want to contribute?

2. What am I passionate about?

3. What are my strengths, gifts, and key abilities?

---

[63]   Stoltzfus, Tony (2008), Coaching Questions: A Coach's Guide to Powerful Asking Skills, Virginia Beach, VA.

Quote of the Day

"The dreams and passions stored within hearts are powerful keys which can unlock a wealth of potential."

~ John C. Maxwell

Job Title: Cyber Ops Planner

Develop detailed plans for the conduct or support of the applicable range of cyber operations through collaboration with other planners, operators, and/or analysts. Participate in targeting selection, validation, and synchronization, and enable integration during the execut on of cyber actions.

Category: Collect and Operate

Specialty Area: Cyber Operational Planning

IT Role Abilities:

- Ab lity to communicate complex information, concepts, or ideas in a confident and well-organized mcnner through verbal, written, and/or visual means.

- Ab lity to accurately and completely source all data used in intelligence, assessment, and/or planning prcducts.

- Ab lity to adjust to and operate in a diverse, unpredictable, challenging, and fast-paced work environment.

- Ab lity to apply approved planning, development, and staffing processes.

- Ab lity to apply critical reading/thinking skills.

- Ab lity to collaborate effectively with others.

- Ab lity to coordinate cyber operations with other orcanization functions or support activities.

- Ability to develop or recommend planning solutions to problems and situations for which no precedent exists.

- Ability to effectively collaborate via virtual teams.

- Ability to exercise judgment when policies are not well-defined.

- Ability to function in a collaborative environment, seeking continuous consultation with other analysts and experts—both internal and external to the organization—to leverage analytical and technical expertise.

- Ability to identify external partners with common cyber operations interests.

- Ability to interpret and apply laws, regulations, policies, and guidance relevant to organization cyber objectives.

- Ability to interpret and understand complex and rapidly-evolving concepts.

- Ability to participate as a member of planning teams, coordination groups, and task forces as necessary.

- Ability to tailor technical and planning information to a customer's level of understanding.

Suggested Education/Work Experience: Bachelor's degree and fourteen years of professional experience, or a master's degree and twelve years of professional experience.

Funding Resources for Training (Scholarships may be available such as these): AIAA Foundation Scholarship Program, Michigan Council of Women in Technology High School Scholarship, Michigan Council of Women in Technology Undergraduate Scholarship, MIT THINK

Scholars Program, National GEM Consortium—MS Engineering Fellowships, National GEM Consortium—PHD Engineering Fellowships

Types of Industry Certifications: Certified Cyber Forensics Professional, Intelligence Planner Certification Program, Global Industrial Cyber Security Professional, Certified Cyber Security Professional, Certified Network Defender, CSX Expert, GIAC Information Security Fundamentals

Possible U.S. Salary Ranges: $81,000-$101,000+

Similar U.S. Industry Job Titles: Cyberspace Operations Planner, Cyber Operational Planner, Cyber Operations Exercise Planner, Staff Cyber Operations Planner, Cyber Intelligence Specialist, Cyber Joint Operation Planner, Operations Security Planner, Information Operations Planner/Scenario Developer

Summary

As you can see, this IT role requires many years of experience and education because of the need to plan and organize different analytical patterns and coordinate with many internal and external stakeholders on a consistent basis. Be prepared to collaborate with team members from all around the world and be able to explain many technical details in language that everyone can understand in the simplest terms possible related to policy, regulations, cyber activities, and other legal terms and conditions that may occur on a regular basis.

Coaching Time[64]

Ask yourself these powerful coaching questions:

1. What has my whole life prepared me to do?

2. What experiences have most shaped who I am as a person? How have those changes prepared me for what I most want to do in my life?

3. "Don't just think work." How can I combine all my experiences from all areas of my life?

4. What kind of role or task would bring all the best of what I have learned in life so far?

Quote of the Day

"You are never too old to set another goal or dream a new dream."

~ C. S. Lewis

---

[64] Stoltzfus, Tony (2008): Coaching Questions, A Coach's Guide to Powerful Asking Skills, Virginia Beach, VA

National Initiative for Cybersecurity Education (NICE) Cybersecurity Workforce Framework

17th NICE Framework IT Role

Job Title: Cyber Policy and Strategy Planner

Develop and maintain cybersecurity plans, strategy, and policy to support and align with organizational cybersecurity initiatives and regulatory compliance.

Category: Oversee and Govern

Specialty Area: Strategic Planning and Policy

IT Role Abilities:

- Ability to determine the validity of technology trend data.

- Ability to develop policy, plans, and strategy in compliance with laws, regulations, policies, and standards in support of organizational cyber activities.

- Ability to leverage best practices and lessons learned of external organizations and academic institutions dealing with cyber issues.

Suggested Education/Work Experience: Bachelor's degree in information systems, computer science, or related fields and 2 years of experience (academic, internship, or professional) in Cyber Security Analysis or related role.

Funding Resources for Training (Scholarships may be available such as these): Truthfinder Scholarship for Women in STEM, Future STEM Teacher Scholarship, ESA Foundation Scholarship, Christian Larew Memorial Scholarship, Morphisecs Women in Cybersecurity Scholarship

Types of Industry Certifications: GIAC Information Security Fundamentals, Certified Cyber Forensics Professional, Intelligence Planner Certification Program, Global Industrial Cyber Security Professional, Certified Cyber Security Professional, The Certified Information Privacy Professional, Certified Network Defender, CompTIA Network+, CompTIA Security+, EC Council Certified Information Security Officer

Possible U.S. Salary Ranges: $27,500-$143,000+

Similar U.S. Industry Job Titles: Cyber Security Policy Analyst, Cyber Security Analyst, Policy Analyst, Cyber Security Governance Analyst, IT Security Analyst, Principle Information Security Analyst, Cyber Information Assurance Analyst, Policy Advisor

Summary

As you can see, this IT role has only a few required abilities, but keep in mind, in this position, you will need to know a lot in many different areas of information technology and cybersecurity activities so your strategic initiatives, plans, and policies are aligned with best practices. Continue to stay abreast of industry trends and technical standards, and try to customize and balance the overall strategies so they can be adhered to and implemented across the IT infrastructure while meeting business needs.

Coaching Time

Ask yourself these powerful coaching questions:

1.   What do I want to learn?

2.   What skills do I want to master?

3.   What have I always wished I could accomplish?

Quote of the Day

"Success is not final; failure is not fatal. It is the courage to continue that counts."

~ Winston S. Churchill

National Initiative for Cybersecurity Education (NICE) Cybersecurity Workforce Framework

18th NICE Framework IT Role

Job Title: Cyber Workforce Developer and Manager

Develop cyberspace workforce plans, strategies, and guidance to support cyberspace workforce manpower, personnel, training, and education requirements, and to address changes to cyberspace policy, doctrine, material, force structure, and education and training requirements.

Category: Oversee and Govern

Specialty Area: Strategic Planning and Policy

IT Role Abilities:

- Ability to design and validate reliable assessments.
- Ability to assess and forecast manpower requirements to meet organizational objectives.
- Ability to develop policy, plans, and strategy in compliance with laws, regulations, policies, and standards in support of organizational cyber activities.
- Ability to leverage best practices and lessons learned of external organizations and academic institutions dealing with cyber issues.
- Ability to develop career path opportunities.
- Ability to determine the validity of workforce trend data.

Suggested Education/Work Experience: Advanced degree or equivalent credits/certifications and 10 years of relevant experience, and be a person who is typically identified as a recognized industry leader.

Funding Resources for Training: (Scholarships may be available such as these): RA Consulting Service/Maria Riley Scholarships, ScienceLogic Scholarship, Innovation in Sales Technology Scholarship, Digital Marketing Scholarship Program, Digital Privacy Scholarship, Samuel S. Wilks Memorial Award

Types of Industry Certifications: Certified Cyber Forensics Professional, Certified Information Privacy Manager, Project Manager, Professional Cloud Security Manager Certification, Certified Manager Certification, Certified Information Security Manager, Certified Information System Security Professional

Possible U.S. Salary Ranges: $46,000-$121,000+

Similar U.S. Industry Job Titles: Policy and Workforce Developer SME, Cybersecurity Design and Engineering Professional, Cybersecurity Officer, IT Security Specialist, Cyber Operations Manager, Deputy Chief Information Security Officer, Talent Acquisition Specialist-Cybersecurity

Summary

As you can see, this IT role may require advanced education, several years of experience, and industry expertise to be the best candidate for this position. If you are considering this role, start to think of how you can add value to the cybersecurity industry through speaking engagements, writing knowledge articles, volunteering at events, joining associations, and obtaining globally-recognized certifications. Try to share your knowledge in ways that help others to improve their cybersecurity posture and you will exceed in this role for years to come.

Coaching Time

Ask yourself these powerful coaching questions:[65]

1. What do I need that I don't have now to make a great decision?

2. Who could I tap to help me make a great decision?

3. What would it cost me if I didn't move forward with this?

Quote of the Day

"Success is achieved in inches, not miles."

~ *John C. Maxwell*

---

[65] Stoltzfus, Tony (2005), Leadership Coaching: The Discipline, Skills and Heart of a Christian Coach.

National Initiative for Cybersecurity Education (NICE) Cybersecurity Workforce Framework

19th NICE Framework IT Role

Job Title: Data Analyst

Examine data from multiple disparate sources with the goal of providing security and privacy insights. Design and implement custom algorithms, workflow processes, and layouts for complex, enterprise-scale data sets used for modeling, data mining, and research purposes.

Category: Operate and Maintain

Specialty Area: Data Administration

IT Role Abilities:

- Ability to build complex data structures and high-level programming languages.

- Ability to dissect a problem and examine the interrelationships between data that may appear unrelated.

- Ability to identify basic common coding flaws at a high level.

- Ability to use data visualization tools (e.g., Flare, HighCharts, AmCharts, D3.js, Processing, Google Visualization API, Tableau, Raphael.js).

- Ability to accurately and completely source all data used in intelligence, assessment, and/or planning products.

Suggested Education/Work Experience: Bachelor's degree may be required and 1 year of experience preferred.

Funding Resources for Training: (Scholarships may be available such as these): CH2M/AEESP Outstanding Doctoral Dissertation Award, IOBSE Scholarships, Industrial Design & Learning Technology Scholarships, Helen J. Sioussat/Fay Wells Scholarship, Crush the PMP Scholarship Program, Dotcom-Monitor Women in Computing Scholarship

Types of Industry Certifications: Certified Health Data Analyst, Data Center Architect, Information System Analyst, Certified Data Management Professional-Data Management, Certified Data Management Administrator, Certified Insurance Data Manager, CompTIA Cloud Essentials, Cloud Architect

Possible U.S. Salary Ranges: $46,000-$96,000+

Similar U.S. Industry Job Titles: Data Analyst, Network Security Specialist, Operations Data Analyst, Associate Cyber Intelligence Analyst, Business Data Analyst, Data Scientist, Data Engineer, Data Security Analytics Analyst

Summary

This IT role is very statistical and analytical, so if you are good in mathematics and computer programming, you will excel in this position. Get familiar with business intelligence software and the latest data visualization tools so you will be ahead of the game in your knowledge, skills, and abilities, and you can hit the ground running on day one and be successful.

Coaching Time[66]

Ask yourself these powerful coaching questions:

1. What obstacles do I need to overcome to reach my goal?

2. If I had unlimited resources and could not fail, what would I do?

3. Is there a step I want to take?

Quote of the Day

"Don't let what you cannot do interfere with what you can do."

~ John Wooden

---

[66]   Stoltzfus, Tony (2005), Leadership Coaching: The Disciplines, Skills, and Heart of a Christian Coach

National Initiative for Cybersecurity Education (NICE) Cybersecurity Workforce Framework

20th NICE Framework IT Role

Job Title: Database Administrator

Administer databases and/or data management systems that allow for the secure storage, query, protection, and utilization of data.

Category: Operate and Maintain

Specialty Area: Data Administration

IT Role Abilities:

- Ability to maintain databases (i.e., backup, restore, delete data, transaction log files, etc.).

Suggested Education/Work Experience: Bachelor's degree in Computer Science or a similar path of education and experience.

Funding Resources for Training (Scholarships may be available such as these): Custom Creatives Digital Marketing Scholarship Program, Herschede Engineering Scholarship, Harold and Inge Marcus Scholarship, Institute of Food Technologists Sophomore Scholarship, Half Chrome Drones Scholarship

Types of Industry Certifications: Database Design Specialists, Oracle Database Cloud Service, Microsoft Database Fundamentals, Certified Data Management Professional-Data Management, MySQL X Developer, Information System Analyst

Possible U.S. Salary Ranges: $46,000-$109,000+

Similar U.S. Industry Job Titles: Principal Database Administrator-IT, Database and Systems Administrator, Temporary Access Database Administrator, SQL Database Administrator, Oracle Database Administrator, MySQL Database Administrator, Microsoft SQL Database Administrator, Database Specialist, Database Analyst

Summary

In this IT role, it is very important to understand best practices for data management and data lifecycle processes and procedures so the business can make informed decisions on the data being maintained. In addition, data analysis, data retrieval, and data retention will be key functions of this role on a day-to-day basis, including knowing the key database operating system functions and commands so data can be turned into valuable information and knowledge that can be acted upon.

Coaching Time

Ask yourself these powerful coaching questions:

1. What have I done in my life that was deeply fulfilling that I would like to do more of?

2. If the perfect opportunity came along, what would it look like?

3. What situation would really fit me—where I felt like I was born to do this? Describe it.

Quote of the Day

"Never forget how wildly capable you are."
~ Author Unknown

National Initiative for Cybersecurity Education (NICE) Cybersecurity Workforce Framework

21ˢᵗ NICE Framework IT Role

Job Title: Enterprise Architect

Develop and maintain business, systems, and information processes to support enterprise mission needs; develop information technology (IT) rules and requirements that describe baseline and target architectures.

Category: Securely Provision

Specialty Area: Systems Architecture

IT Role Abilities:

- Ability to apply the methods, standards, and approaches for describing, analyzing, and documenting an organization's enterprise information technology (IT) architecture (e.g., The Open Group Architecture Framework [TOGAF], Department of Defense Architecture Framework [DoDAF], Federal Enterprise Architecture Framework [FEAF]).

- Ability to conduct vulnerability scans and recognize vulnerabilities in security systems.

- Ability to apply an organization's goals and objectives to develop and maintain architecture.

- Ability to optimize systems to meet enterprise performance requirements.

- Ability to execute technology integration processes.

- Ability to build architectures and frameworks.

- Ability to apply cybersecurity and privacy principles to organizational requirements (relevant to confidentiality, integrity, availability, authentication, non-repudiation).

- Ability to identify critical infrastructure systems with information communication technologies that were designed without system security considerations.

- Ability to set up a physical or logical sub-network that separates an internal local area network (LAN) from other untrusted networks.

Suggested Education/Work Experience: Bachelor of Arts or Bachelor of Science degree, and 2-5 years of hands-on architecture development experience using DoDAF.

Funding Resources for Training (Scholarships may be available such as these): Gertrude M. Cox Scholarship, Anne Friedberg Innovative Scholarship Award, Business Leaders of Tomorrow, JMJ Phillip Group College Scholarship, Proven Data Recovery Technology Scholarships

Types of Industry Certifications: Enterprise Architect, Senior Enterprise Architect, Enterprise Architect Fellow, Distinguished Enterprise Architect, The Open Group Architect Framework, Data Center Architect, Cloud Architect, Certified Network Defense Architect, GIAC Certified Enterprise Defender, Professional Cloud Solutions Architect Certification, Certified in the Governance of Enterprise IT

Possible U.S. Salary Ranges: $53,000-$268,000+

Similar U.S. Industry Job Titles: Enterprise Architect, Process Architect, Enterprise Data Architect, Cloud Architect, Junior Enterprise Architect, Enterprise Architect Specialist, Enterprise Analytics Architect Lead, Enterprise BI Architect, Senior Solutions/Enterprise Architect, Enterprise Architect Analyst, Network Architect Intermediate, IT Enterprise Architect, Enterprise Cybersecurity Architect

This IT role is crucial and very technically advanced, so you will need to have a clear understanding of the different IT architecture frameworks, policies, and baseline rules so you can build a secure and robust infrastructure that will be sustainable, resilient, and meets the business needs for capacity.

Summary

As you can see with this role, the salary range is extremely lucrative and wide-ranging, and will depend on the size of the company you work for and the type of industry. The more hands-on experience you gain the better your chances will be to land the best job and obtain the salary range you desire. Be familiar with different cloud architectures and obtain the necessary IT certifications.

Coaching Time

Ask yourself these powerful coaching questions:

1.   What options can I create?

2.   If I had a choice, what would it be?

3.   What is going to be my game plan moving forward?

Quote of the Day

"Follow your bliss and the universe will open doors for you where there were only walls."

~ Joseph Campbell

National Initiative for Cybersecurity Education (NICE) Cybersecurity Workforce Framework

22nd NICE Framework IT Role

Job Title: Executive Cyber Leadership

Execute decision-making authorities and establish vision and direction for an organization's cyber and cyber-related resources and/or operations.

Category: Oversee and Govern

Specialty Area: Executive Cyber Leadership

IT Role Abilities:

- Ability to develop policies, plans, and strategies in compliance with laws, regulations, policies, and standards in support of organizational cyber activities.

- Ability to apply critical reading/thinking skills.

- Ability to exercise judgment when policies are not well-defined.

- Ability to interpret and apply laws, regulations, policies, and guidance relevant to organization cyber objectives.

- Ability to tailor technical and planning information to a customer's level of understanding.

- Ability to think critically.

- Ability to prioritize and allocate cybersecurity resources correctly and efficiently.

- Ability to relate strategy, business, and technology in the context of organizational dynamics.

- Ability to understand technology, management, and leadership issues related to organization processes and problem solving.

- Ability to understand the basic concepts and issues related to cyber and its organizational impact.

- Ability to ensure information security management processes are integrated with strategic and operational planning processes.

- Ability to ensure that senior officials within the organization provide information security for the information and systems that support the operations and assets under their control.

Suggested Education/Work Experience: BA or BS degree in Computer Science, Information Security, or Information Systems, and 10+ years of experience with leadership roles in cyber defense areas, including cyber-threat intelligence, detection, incident response, and detection engineering.

Funding Resources for Training (Scholarships may be available such as these): Best Foot Forward Scholarship, Employment Boost College Scholarship, ASCLD Scholarship Program, Generation III Scholarship, eLearners Online College Scholarship

Types of Industry Certifications: Certified Information System Security Professional, EC Council Certified Chief Information Security Officer, GIAC Security Leadership Certification, Certified Information Security Manager, Global Industrial Cyber Security Professional, Certified Cyber Security Professional, CSX Expert, Information System Security Management Professional

Possible U.S. Salary Ranges: $153,858-$380,000+

Similar U.S. Industry Job Titles: Cybersecurity Strategist, Chief Information Security Officer, Cyber Defense Executive, Chief Information Officer, Cyber Security Director, Information Security Officer

Summary

As you can see in this IT role, you will need to have leadership skills and executive presence, and have a strategic point of view in order to manage your cybersecurity program. This leadership role pays very well and can be an extremely fast-paced and time-consuming role. You need to be prepared to work hard and be available at the ready when a new issue arises. Be prepared to have those late-night phone calls because hackers are on the prowl at all hours of the day and night. This job may sometimes be stressful and satisfying at the same time, so be flexible and ready for the challenge.

Coaching Time

Ask yourself these powerful coaching questions:

1. In the bigger scheme of things, how important is this?

2. What would it cost me if I didn't move forward with this opportunity?

3. What is my conclusion?

Quote of the Day

"There is faith in the future and power in the present."

~ *Eckhart Tolle*

National Initiative for Cybersecurity Education (NICE) Cybersecurity Workforce Framework

23rd NICE Framework IT Role

Job Title: Exploitation Analyst

Collaborate to identify access and collection gaps that can be satisfied through cyber collection and/or preparation activities. Leverage all authorized resources and analytic techniques to penetrate targeted networks.

Category: Analyze

Specialty Area: Exploitation Analysis

IT Role Abilities:

- Ability to communicate complex information, concepts, or ideas in a confident and well-organized manner through verbal, written, and/or visual means.

- Ability to accurately and completely source all data used in intelligence, assessment, and/or planning products.

- Ability to collaborate effectively with others.

- Ability to develop or recommend analytic approaches or solutions to problems and situations for which information is incomplete or for which no precedent exists.

- Ability to evaluate, analyze, and synthesize large quantities of data (which may be fragmented and contradictory) into high-quality, fused-targeting/intelligence products.

- Ability to expand network access by conducting target analysis and collection to identify targets of interest.

- Ability to identify/describe target vulnerability.

- Ability to identify/describe techniques/methods for conducting technical exploitation of the target.

- Ability to select the appropriate implant to achieve operational goals.

Suggested Education/Work Experience: Bachelor's degree or Master's degree in Cyber Security, Computer Science, Information Security, or other related fields is preferred, and 2-4 years of relevant experience and/or consulting in the private sector are a major plus.

Funding Resources for Training (Scholarships may be available such as these): Lemelson Center Fellowships, Barnes W. Rose, Jr. and Eva Rose Nichol Scholarship Fund, The Bee Winkler Weinstein Scholarship Fund, Crush the GMAT Scholarship Program, Crush the LSAT Scholarship Program, Crush the GRE Scholarship Program

Types of Industry Certifications: GIAC Certified Intrusion Analyst, Information System Analyst, GIAC Network Forensic Analyst, EC-Council Certified Security Analyst, CompTIA Cybersecurity Analyst, Systems Security Certified Practitioner, Information Technology Security Fundamentals, Certified Information System Security Professional, The Certified Information Privacy Professional, CompTIA Security +, Certified Network Computer Technician, GIAC Security Leadership Certification

Possible U.S. Salary Ranges: $19,000-$147,000+

Similar U.S. Industry Job Titles: IT Security Analyst (Network), Computer Network Analyst, Penetration Tester, Digital Forensic and Incident Response Analyst, Offensive Security Analyst, Senior Security Analyst (Cyber Investigations), Cybersecurity Analyst, Cybersecurity

Computer Network Defense Analyst, IT Security Specialist (Cyber Defense Forensic Analyst), Mobile Exploitation Analyst, Cyber Threat Intelligence Analyst, Information Security Analyst, Cybersecurity Network Analyst

Summary

This IT role is very analytical, and you will be required to evaluate and synthesize vast amounts of fragmented data. Be prepared to present and communicate your findings to management on a regular basis so all interested parties stay informed on the status of its information assets and infrastructure capabilities. Always stay on top of new network devices, cyber threats, and new exploits so you are prepared at any given time to protect and defend the IT environment.

Coaching Time

Ask yourself these powerful coaching questions:

1. What will I take away from this?

2. How can I pull this all together?

3. How do I envision this will work out?

Quote of the Day

"You were born to win, but to be a winner, you must plan to win, prepare to win, and expect to win."

~ Zig Ziglar

National Initiative for Cybersecurity Education (NICE) Cybersecurity Workforce Framework

24th NICE Framework IT Role

Job Title: IT Investment/Portfolio Manager

Manage a portfolio of IT investments that align with the overall needs of mission and enterprise priorities.

Category: Oversee and Govern

Specialty Area: Program/Project Management and Acquisition

IT Role Abilities:

- Ability to oversee the development and update of the life-cycle cost estimate.

Suggested Education/Work Experience: Bachelor's degree plus 3+ years of Financial Management and Information Technology experience.

Funding Resources for Training (Scholarships may be available such as these): Tech Mastery Scholarships, Murrietta Circuits Scholarships Opportunity, Scholarship for Women Business, Alwin B. Newton Scholarship, AIP State Department Fellowship, Public Health Informatics Fellowship Program (PHIFP)

Types of Industry Certifications: Portfolio Management Professional, Certified Manager, Certified Technology Manager, Certified IT Consultant, Certified Senior Technology Manager, Master Project Manager, Certified Information Security Manager, GIAC Certified Project Manager, Certified in Governance of Enterprise IT, Certified Defense Financial Manager, Certified Information System Security Professional

Possible U.S. Salary Ranges: $75,000-$187,000+

Similar U.S. Industry Job Titles: IT Infrastructure Project Manager, Portfolio Manager, IT Security Manager, IT Portfolio Analyst, IT Product Portfolio Manager, IT Delivery Manager, Information Technology Specialist, Infrastructure Portfolio Manager, IT Project Manager, IT Program Manager, IT Operations Portfolio Manager

Summary

As you can see, this IT role will be responsible for the overall portfolio of investments in information assets, including the financial planning and budgeting of the cyber program. Be prepared to fight for the money and to show proven examples of the value of any new and existing assets needed for the organization. Remember to be a good steward of all monies entrusted to you with honesty, integrity, and trustworthiness, so you will have an even greater chance of receiving more money for future projects.

Coaching Time

Ask yourself these powerful coaching questions:

1. What are the best ways for me to support myself at this point?

2. In the past, what has worked for me? What did I learn from that?

3. How will I measure my progress using what I have learned?

Quote of the Day

"The distance between dreams and reality is called action."

~ Author Unknown

National Initiative for Cybersecurity Education (NICE) Cybersecurity Workforce Framework

25th NICE Framework IT Role

Job Title: IT Program Auditor

Conduct evaluations of an IT program or its individual components to determine compliance with published standards.

IT Role Abilities:

- Ability to ensure security practices are followed throughout the acquisition process.

Category: Oversee and Govern

Specialty Area: Program/Project Management and Acquisition

Suggested Education/Work Experience[67]: Bachelor's degree in Accounting, Business, or Finance, and 1-3 years of experience in an Accounting or Auditing role; strong analytical skills and attention to detail preferred.

Funding Resources for Training (Scholarships may be available such as these): 5 Minute Scholarship, Academic Hero Scholarship, Litherland/FTEE Undergraduate Scholarship, Science Mathematics AND Research for Transformation Scholarship, Imagine America College Scholarship for High School Students, The Adelle and Erwin Tomash Fellowship in the History of Information

---

[67] https://www.indeed.com

Types of Industry Certifications[68]: Certified in Risk Management Assurance, Associate in Information Technology, Certified IT Consultant, Certified Business Continuity Lead Auditor, Certified Internal Auditor, Information Technology Security, Certified Information Systems Auditor, CompTIA Project+, Professional Cloud Security Manager Certification, Certified Network Defense Architect, Certified Data Management Professional-Data Management, Certified Information Privacy Manager, Information System Analyst

Possible U.S. Salary Ranges[69]: $54,000-$105,000+

Similar U.S. Industry Job Titles[70]: Information Technology Auditor, Senior IT Auditor-Internal, Staff IT Auditor, Inspector General IT Auditor, IT Security Compliance Analyst, IT Audit Specialist, IT Security Analyst, Director IT Security, IT Specialist, IT Security Auditor/ Cyber Security Auditor, Lead IT Cyber Security Analyst, IT Auditor Entry Level, Corporate IT Auditor, Internal Audit IT Staff Auditor

Summary

In this IT role, you will be tasked with understanding policies, processes, and best-practice industry standards, including those laws that govern the program. You will also need to be prepared to evaluate how the company is measuring up compared to those same standards and other businesses, including standards of due care and due diligence.

As you can see, one of the preferred skill sets to have is being able to pay close attention to detail, and being able to offer critical feedback and recommendations for

---

[68]   https://www.careeronestop.org/

[69]   https://www.glassdoor.com/Salaries/it-auditor-salary-SRCH_KO0,10.htm

[70]   https://www.indeed.com/

improving the program. Remember to stay up-to-date and on top of new and existing rules and regulations as it relates to information privacy and security and other bodies of knowledge for that company's sector of business.

Coaching Time[71]

Ask yourself these powerful coaching questions:

1. What matters the most to me concerning my work values?

2. How could this value help me, and my team achieve its mission?

3. Which possible pathway do I feel prepared to go down?

Quote of the Day

"The beginning is the most important part of any work."

~ *Plato*

---

[71]   https://positivepsychology.com/life-coaching-questions/

National Initiative for Cybersecurity Education (NICE) Cybersecurity Workforce Framework

26th NICE Framework IT Role

Job Title: IT Project Manager

Directly manage information technology projects.

Category: Oversee and Govern

Specialty Area: Program/Project Management and Acquisition

IT Role Abilities:

- Ability to apply supply chain risk management standards.

- Ability to oversee the development and update of the life-cycle cost estimate.

- Ability to evaluate/ensure the trustworthiness of the supplier and/or product.

- Ability to ensure security practices are followed throughout the acquisition process.

Suggested Education/Work Experience[72]**:** Bachelor's degree in Business Administration, Computer Science, or related degree, and/or a minimum of 5 years of experience in developing strategies that move technology projects forward, setting goals, creating and implementing action plans, and evaluating the process and results.

---

[72] https://www.indeed.com

Funding Resources for Training (Scholarships may be available such as these): American Express Professional Development Scholarship, ASLMS Student Research Grants, NSPS Berntsen International Scholarship in Surveying Technology, PLUS Foundation Financial Aid Scholarship

Types of Industry Certifications[73]: Certified IT Consultant, Professional Cloud Security Manager Certification, Master Project Manager, Certified Information Security Manager, Project Management Professional, GIAC Certified Project Manager, Information Technology Security, Certified International Project Manager, Certified Business Professional-Project Management

Possible U.S. Salary Ranges[74]: $61,000-$130,000+

Similar U.S. Industry Job Titles[75]: Project Manager, Project Manager-IT Infrastructure, IT Project Manager-Supply Chain, IT Project Inter Manager, IT Infrastructure Project Manager, Program Manager, IT Senior Project Manager, IT Professional/Project Manager, IT Project Manager-Cybersecurity, IT Project Manager/Business Analyst

Summary

As you can see in this IT role, you will be responsible for setting goals and managing the life cycle of the project to its completion. Be strategic and set time-bound tasks with deadlines that get results that are realistic and measurable for all involved parties. Keep leaders abreast of your project milestones, deadlines, and

---

[73]   https://www.careeronestop.org/

[74]   https://www.glassdoor.com/Salaries/project-manager-salary-SRCH_KO0,15.htm

[75]   https://www.indeed.com/

accomplishments, and build security practices in on the front end to avoid issues in the future.

Coaching Time[76]

Ask yourself these powerful coaching questions:

1. How do I feel I could best motivate myself?

2. What are the best ways for me to support myself at this point?

3. If I had no restrictions at all, who would I be?

Quote of the Day

"It is never too late to be what you might have been."

~ George Eliot

---

[76]   https://positivepsychology.com/life-coaching-questions/

National Initiative for Cybersecurity Education (NICE) Cybersecurity Workforce Framework

27th NICE Framework IT Role

Job Title: Information Systems Security Developer

Design, develop, test, and evaluate information system security throughout the systems development life cycle.

Category: Securely Provision

Specialty Area: Systems Development

IT Role Abilities:

- Ability to identify systemic security issues based on the analysis of vulnerability and configuration data.

- Ability to apply the methods, standards, and approaches for describing, analyzing, and documenting an organization's enterprise information technology (IT) architecture (e.g., The Open Group Architecture Framework [TOGAF], Department of Defense Architecture Framework [DoDAF], Federal Enterprise Architecture Framework [FEAF]).

- Ability to ask clarifying questions.

- Ability to communicate complex information, concepts, or ideas in a confident and well-organized manner through verbal, written, and/or visual means.

- Ability to conduct vulnerability scans and recognize vulnerabilities in security systems.

- Ability to produce technical documentation.

- Ability to analyze test data.

- Ability to translate data and test results into evaluative conclusions.

- Ability to apply network security architecture concepts including topology, protocols, components, and principles (e.g., application of defense-in-depth).

- Ability to apply secure system design tools, methods, and techniques.

- Ability to apply system design tools, methods, and techniques, including automated systems analysis and design tools.

- Ability to ensure security practices are followed throughout the acquisition process.

- Ability to design architectures and frameworks.

- Ability to collaborate effectively with others.

- Ability to function in a collaborative environment, seeking continuous consultation with other analysts and experts—both internal and external to the organization—to leverage analytical and technical expertise.

- Ability to participate as a member of planning teams, coordination groups, and task forces as necessary.

- Ability to understand objectives and effects.

- Ability to understand the basic concepts and issues related to cyber and its organizational impact.

- Ability to apply cybersecurity and privacy principles to organizational requirements (relevant to confidentiality, integrity, availability, authentication, and non-repudiation).

- Ability to identify critical infrastructure systems with information communication technology that were designed without system security considerations.

Suggested Education/Work Experience[77]: A degree in Computer Science, Mathematics, or other technical discipline (equivalent experience may be acceptable). Some understanding of general information security concepts and principles, system architectures and development, network protocols, etc., and general programming and software analysis skills.

Funding Resources for Training (Scholarships may be available such as these): Society of Women Engineers Scholarship, National Honor Society State Scholarships, Myrtle & Earl Walker Scholarships, L'Oréal USA For Women in Science Fellowship, Artificial Intelligence & Ethics Scholarship, Live Career Education Opportunities Scholarship

Types of Industry Certifications[78]: Certified Cloud Security Professional, Associate of International Information System Security Certification Consortium, Certified Information Privacy Technologist, Certification in Risk and Information System Control, The Certified Information Privacy Professional, System Security Certified Practitioner, GIAC Security Leadership Certification, GIAC Information Security Professional

Possible U.S. Salary Ranges[79]: $21,000-$135,000+

Similar U.S. Industry Job Titles[80]: Software Engineer-Analyst (IT Security Consultant), Project Manager-Analyst IT, System Analyst-Security, Information Technology-Cybersecurity, Information System Security Officer, IT Enterprise System Developer, Information Security-

---

77   https://www.indeed.com
78   https://www.careeronestop.org/
79   https://www.glassdoor.com/Salaries/information-systems-security-engineer-salary-SRCH_KO0,37.htm
80   https://www.indeed.com/

Cybersecurity Analyst, Deputy Chief Information Security Officer, Senior Information Assurance Associate, IT Systems Administrator, Information Technology Specialist, Senior Systems Administrator, IT Security Analyst, Information Security Auditor-Expert

Summary

As you can see with this IT role, it would be best to understand the information system lifecycle, architecture, and design of the environment. Secure coding and vulnerability management will need to be understood so that the infrastructure is reliable and sustainable and meets business capacity requirements. Finding the right security baseline and managing for threat and IT risks will be key to success.

Coaching Time[81]

Ask yourself these powerful coaching questions:

1. What positive things do I feel will happen if I accomplish what I am trying to achieve?

2. How will I know if I have attained my desired outcome?

Quote of the Day

"In the matters of style, swim with the current. In the matters of principle, stand like a rock."

~ *Thomas Jefferson*

---

[81] https://positivepsychology.com/life-coaching-questions/

National Initiative for Cybersecurity Education (NICE) Cybersecurity Workforce Framework

28th NICE Framework IT Role

Job Title: Information Systems Security Manager

Responsible for the cybersecurity cf a program, organization, system, or enclave.

Category: Oversee and Govern

Specialty Area: Cybersecurity Management

IT Role Abilities:

- Ability to apply techniques for detecting host and network-based intrusions using intrusion detection technologies.

- Ability to integrate information security requirements into the acquisition process, using applicable baseline security controls as one of the sources for security requirements, ensuring a robust software quality control process, and establishing multiple sources (e.g., delivery routes) for critical system elements.

- Ability to identify critical infrastructure systems with information communication technology that were designed without system security considerations.

Suggested Education/Work Experience[82]: Bachelor's degree in Computer Science, Information Technology, Computer Engineering, or related degree; *or,* an associate degree with 2 years of experience; *or,* 4 years of basic to intermediate level computer hardware-related experience.

---

[82] https://www.indeed.com

Funding Resources for Training (Scholarships may be available such as these): Phi Upsilon Omicron Challenge Scholarship, Isabel M. Herson Scholarship in Education, FCBA Foundation College Scholarship Program, ASEE/NSF Small Business Postdoctoral Research Diversity Fellowship, Elizabeth M. Gruber Scholarship

Types of Industry Certifications[83]: GIAC Information Security Professional, Certified Cloud Security Professional, Information Security Analyst, Associate of International Information Systems Security Certification Consortium, Certified Information Privacy Technologist, Certification in Risk and Information Systems Control, The Certified Information Privacy Professional, Systems Security Certified Practitioner, GIAC Security Leadership Certification, Certified Information Systems Security Professional, Certified Information Security Manager

Possible U.S. Salary Ranges[84]: $69,000-$130,000+

Similar U.S. Industry Job Titles[85]: IT Manager (Information Security), Information Security (Technical Manager), Cyber Security (Information Security Manager), Manager (Information Security Risk), Director Information Security (Cyber Risk Management), Information Security Manager, Senior Manager IT Security Operations, Information Systems Security Manager, Director of Information Technology and Security

Summary

As you can see with this IT role, it is more of a management position where the individual will oversee

---

[83] https://www.careeronestop.org/
[84] https://www.payscale.com/research/US/Job=Information_
      Systems_Security Manager/Salary
[85] https://www.indeed.com/

and direct the governance of a team or program. Also, incident management may be a key function of this role, in addition to the critical tasks of securing the information system controls and the mitigating of vulnerabilities of the infrastructure. Be mindful that there is a minimum requirement of 4 years of work experience or an associate degree with 2 years of experience, but having a plan in place to get a 4-year degree is crucial so that you have a better chance of growing on the leadership track in the foreseeable future.

Coaching Time[86]

Ask yourself these powerful coaching questions:

1. What am I afraid of that's getting in the way of living the life I want?

2. What am I ready to change?

3. What am I NOT ready to change YET?

Quote of the Day

"Never give up on the person you are becoming."

~ Anonymous

---

[86]   549 Powerful Coaching Questions
www.thecoachingtoolscompany.com

National Initiative for Cybersecurity Education (NICE) Cybersecurity Workforce Framework

29th NICE Framework IT Role

Job Title: Knowledge Manager

Responsible for the management and administration of processes and tools that enable the organization to identify, document, and access intellectual capital and information content.

Category: Operate and Maintain

Specialty Area: Knowledge Management

IT Role Abilities:

- Ability to match the appropriate knowledge repository technology for a given application or environment.

Suggested Education/Work Experience[87]: Bachelor's degree and 3+ years of experience in Cyber Security preferred.

Funding Resources for Training[88] (Scholarships may be available such as these): AISES Oracle Academy Scholarship, Everett Oscar Shimp Memorial Scholarships, Astronaut Scholarship Foundation Scholarship, Eugene Garfield Doctoral Dissertation Fellowship, Netfloor USA Access Flooring College Scholarships

---

[87] https://www.indeed.com

[88] www.careeronestop.org

Types of Industry Certifications[89]: Certified Information Security Manager, Certified International Project Manager, Certified in Quality/Organizational Excellence, CompTIA Project+, Software Configuration Management, GIAC Security Leadership Certification, GIAC Information Security Professional, Certified Associate in Project Management, IT Infrastructure Library Certification

Possible U.S. Salary Ranges[90]**:** $48,000-$119,000+

Similar U.S. Industry Job Titles[91]**:** Cyber Operations Technical Manager, Program Manager, IT Program Manager, Manager (Platform Engineer), Technical Program Manager, Information Technology Project Manager, Business Analyst

Summary

In this IT role, knowledge of the information and infrastructure is essential to the position. It will be helpful to be well-organized and resourceful so finding and accessing the data you will need will be easily retrievable and manageable. Creating knowledge articles for recurring tasks will be helpful and will save time when the situation or incident happens in the future.

---

[89]   https://www.careeronestop.org/
[90]   https://www.payscale.com/research/US/Job=Knowledge_
       Manager/Salary
[91]   https://www.indeed.com/

Coaching Time[92]

Ask yourself these powerful coaching questions:

1. What do I stand for?

2. What would I stand up and fight for?

3. What will I risk my reputation over?

Quote of the Day

"In life you have 3 choices, give up, give in, or give it your all."

~ *Charleston Parker*

---

[92] 549 Powerful Coaching Questions
www.thecoachingtoolscompany.com

National Initiative for Cybersecurity Education (NICE) Cybersecurity Workforce Framework

30th NICE Framework IT Role

Job Title: Law Enforcement/Counterintelligence Forensics Analyst

Conduct detailed investigations on computer-based crimes, establishing documentary or physical evidence to include digital media and logs associated with cyber intrusion incidents.

Category: Investigate

Specialty Area: Digital Forensics

IT Role Abilities:

- Ability to decrypt digital data collections.

- Ability to examine digital media on multiple operating system platforms.

Suggested Education/Work Experience[93]: The selected candidate must have experience with all-source analysis and/or data analytics and a working knowledge of counterintelligence principles and objectives. Candidate shall be highly motivated and passionate about the mission.

Funding Resources for Training (Scholarships may be available such as these): Technology First/Robert V. McKenna Scholarship, PolicyPak Scholarship, Print and Graphic Scholarship Foundation Awards, University of the Aftermarket Foundation Scholarship, REFORMA Scholarship

---

93   https://www.indeed.com

Types of Industry Certifications[94]: Certified Law Enforcement Analyst, Criminal Intelligence Certified Analyst, GIAC Certified Forensics Examiner, Certified Cyber Forensics Professional, GIAC Certified Forensics Analyst, Professional Certified Investigator

Possible U.S. Salary Ranges: $48,000-$116,000+

Similar U.S. Industry Job Titles[95]*:* Intelligence Analyst, Intelligence Specialist, Cyber Security Analyst, Security Analyst, Intelligence Operations Specialist, Special Agent, Counter-Intelligence Agent, SOC Analyst, Information Security Specialist, Field Investigator, Insider Threat Cyber Intelligence Analyst, NSA Police Officer, Inspector General Criminal Investigator, Senior Digital Forensics Analyst

Summary

As you can see with this IT role, it will be helpful to know how to perform computer-based forensics and know how encryption and decryption of data in-transit and at-rest works. Be familiar with how the chain-of-custody handling procedures work for evidence, and it can help a lot on rough days to be passionate about the organization's mission to protect and serve its people. Also having a great work ethic and a defender personality and mindset will go a long way in helping you do your job extremely well each day.

Coaching Time[96]

Ask yourself these powerful coaching questions:

---

[94] https://www.payscale.com/research/US/Job=Forensic_Computer_Analyst/Salary
[95] https://www.indeed.com/
[96] 549 Powerful Coaching Questions
www.thecoachingtoolscompany.com

1.   What obstacles do I expect to meet?

2.   What are 3 things I could do to support myself to make sure what I want gets done?

3.   What resources do I already have to help me achieve my goals?

Quote of the Day

"You can do it if you believe you can."

~ *Napoleon Hill*

National Initiative for Cybersecurity Education (NICE) Cybersecurity Workforce Framework

31st NICE Framework IT Role

Job Title: Mission Assessment Specialist

Develop assessment plans and measures of performance/effectiveness. Conduct strategic and operational effectiveness assessments as required for cyber events. Determine whether systems performed as expected and provide input to the determination of operational effectiveness.

Category: Analyze

Specialty Area: All-Source Analysis

IT Role Abilities:

- Ability to communicate complex information, concepts, or ideas in a confident and well-organized manner through verbal, written, and/or visual means.

- Ability to accurately and completely source all data used in intelligence, assessment and/or planning products.

- Ability to clearly articulate intelligence requirements into well-formulated research questions and data-tracking variables for inquiry-tracking purposes.

- Ability to develop or recommend analytic approaches or solutions to problems and situations for which information is incomplete or for which no precedent exists.

- Ability to effectively collaborate via virtual teams.

- Ability to evaluate information for reliability, validity, and relevance.

- Ability to evaluate, analyze, and synthesize large quantities of data (which may be fragmented and contradictory) into high-quality, fused-targeting/ intelligence products.

- Ability to exercise judgment when policies are not well-defined.

- Ability to focus research efforts to meet the customer's decision-making needs.

- Ability to function effectively in a dynamic, fast-paced environment.

- Ability to function in a collaborative environment, seeking continuous consultation with other analysts and experts—both internal and external to the organization—to leverage analytical and technical expertise.

- Ability to identify intelligence gaps.

- Ability to recognize and mitigate cognitive biases which may affect analysis.

- Ability to recognize and mitigate deception in reporting and analysis.

- Ability to think critically.

- Ability to think like threat actors.

- Ability to understand objectives and effects.

- Ability to utilize multiple intelligence sources across all intelligence disciplines.

Suggested Education/Work Experience[97]: Bachelor's degree or equivalent military education and/or directly related experience.

---

[97] https://www.indeed.com

Funding Resources for Training (Scholarships may be available such as these): Faye Lynn Roberts Education Scholarship Fund, Shred Nations Scholarship, Mathematics Mentoring Travel Grants, Jack M. Nagasaka Memorial Scholarship, MLA/NLM Spectrum Scholarship, Barriger—Zachary Barriger Memorial Scholarship Fund, Astronaut Scholarship Foundation Scholarship

Types of Industry Certifications[98]: Associate Professional Risk Manager, Certification Internal Control Self Assessments, GIAC Certified ISO-27000 Specialist, Certified Encryption Specialist, Certified Fiber Optic Specialist/Design, Broadband Telecom Center Specialist, Broadband Distribution Specialist, Certified Fiber Optic Specialist/Testing, Certified Criminal Justice Specialist, Certified Security Specialist

Possible U.S. Salary Ranges[99]: $35,000-$90,000+

Similar U.S. Industry Job Titles[100]: Mission Support Specialist, Mission Systems Specialist, Investigations and Inquiries Specialist, Technical Information Specialist, Management Support Specialist, Intelligence Operations Specialist, Intelligence Research Specialist, Intelligence Specialist, Security Specialist, Supervisory Mission Support Specialist, Computer Security Specialist, Operations Specialist, Special Agent, Military Operations Analyst, Information Assurance Compliance Specialist

---

[98]   https://www.careeronestop.org/
[99]   https://www.payscale.com/research/US/Job=Assessment
       _Specialist/Salary
[100]   https://www.indeed.com/

Summary

In this IT role, there will be a lot of critical thinking, gap-analysis measures and mission-driven strategic work involved. There will be times when all the necessary information needed to decide what to do next may not be available, so you will have to be innovative and creative for those instances. Just remember to continuously learn new skills, strategies, and techniques, and keep being proactive in your pursuits to protect the reputation and brand of your organization and its critical assets.

Coaching Time[101]

Ask yourself these powerful coaching questions:

1.   What is my dream for this lifetime?

2.   If there is an outcome that I am secretly looking for, what is it?

3.   How can I make this something I am aiming toward, rather than something I am trying to move away from?

Quote of the Day

"Action is the foundational key to all success."

~ Pablo Picasso

---

[101]   549 Powerful Coaching Questions
www.thecoachingtoolscompany.com

Job Title: Multi-Disciplined Language Analyst

Apply language and cultural expertise with target/threat and technical knowledge to process, analyze, and/or disseminate intelligence information derived from language, voice, and/or graphic material. Create and maintain language-specific databases and working aids to support cyber action execution and ensure critical knowledge sharing. Provide subject matter expertise in foreign-language-intensive or interdisciplinary projects.

Category: Analyze

Specialty Area: Language Analysis

IT Role Abilities:

- Ability to communicate complex information, concepts, or ideas in a confident and well-organized manner through verbal, written, and/or visual means.

- Ability to apply language and cultural expertise to analysis.

- Ability to function in a collaborative environment, seeking continuous consultation with other analysts and experts—both internal and external to the organization—to leverage analytical and technical expertise.

- Ability to review processed target language materials for accuracy and completeness.

Suggested Education/Work Experience[102]:   Minimum Education Requirements (one of the following)

- High school plus 10 years' experience.

- Associate degree plus 10 years' experience.

- Bachelor's degree plus 7 years' experience.

- Desired requirement: Master's degree plus 5 years' experience.

Funding Resources for Training (Scholarships may be available such as these): AHETEMS/ExxonMobil Scholarships, Tech Mastery Scholarships, Claude B. Hart Memorial Scholarship, AFCEA STEM Teacher Graduate Scholarships, Carnegie Observatories Graduate Research Fellowships, Luis W. Alvarez Postdoctoral Fellowship in Computational Science, Boeing Company Scholarship

Types of Industry Certifications[103]: Certified Associate Business Analyst, Certified Software Quality Analyst, Certified Software Business Analyst, Certified Quality Process Analyst, Certified Record Analyst, Certified Marketing Analyst, IQBBA Business Analyst Certification, GIAC Mobile Device Security Analyst, Criminal Intelligence Certified Analyst, Certified User Experience Analyst, EC-Council Certified Security Analyst, GIAC Certified Detection Analyst, Certified Web Analyst

Possible U.S. Salary Ranges[104]: $30,000-$101,000+

Similar U.S. Industry Job Titles[105]: Multi-Disciplined Language Analyst, Principled Intelligence Analyst,

---

[102] https://www.indeed.com
[103] https://www.careeronestop.org/
[104] https://www.payscale.com/research/US/Job=Language_ Analyst/Salary
[105] https://www.indeed.com/https://www.indeed.com/

Technical Lead, Business Analyst, Operational Research Program Manager, Senior Principal Intelligence Analyst

Summary

As you can see in this IT role, the more years of experience you have, the less education or college degrees needed, and the more college degrees you have, the less experience that may be required to get the job. I believe in education, and as a career professional, I believe we need to continuously learn and grow in order to stay in demand and obtain new roles that advance us and challenge our abilities. So, continue to grow in your knowledge and do not be afraid to try new things and fail because that is how you grow.

Coaching Time[106]

Ask yourself these powerful coaching questions:

1. What would I do if I did not have to live with the consequences?

2. So which choice do I like the best?

3. Which decision would be the quickest to complete in order to move forward?

Quote of the Day

"Too much of a good thing can be truly wonderful."

~ Mae West

---

[106] 549 Powerful Coaching Questions
www.thecoachingtoolscompany.com

National Initiative for Cybersecurity Education (NICE) Cybersecurity Workforce Framework

33rd NICE Framework IT Role

Job Title: Network Operations Specialist

Plan, implement, and operate network services/systems, to include hardware and virtual environments.

Category: Operate and Maintain

Specialty Area: Network Services

IT Role Abilities[107]:

- Ability to operate network equipment, including hubs, routers, switches, bridges, servers, transmission media, and related hardware.

- Ability to operate common network tools (e.g., ping, traceroute, nslookup).

  Ability to execute OS command line (e.g., ipconfig, netstat, dir, nbtstat).

- Ability to operate the organization's LAN/WAN pathways.

- Ability to monitor measures or indicators of system performance and availability.

- Ability to operate different electronic communication systems and methods (e.g., e-mail, VCIP, IM, web forums, direct video broadcasts).

- Ability to monitor traffic flows across the network.

- Ability to interpret the information collected by network tools (e.g., nslookup, ping, and traceroute).

---

[107] https://www.indeed.com

Suggested Education/Work Experience: Network administration with 2 years' experience is preferred.

Funding Resources for Training (Scholarships may be available such as these): Stevens Doctoral Award, Women Techmakers Udacity Scholarship, "A Better World" Spirituality and Technology Advancement Scholarship, Tocris Scholarship Program, Capital Auto Auction Annual Scholarship, MIE Solutions Scholarship Opportunity

Types of Industry Certifications[108]: Broadband Telecom Center Specialist, Wireshark Certified Network Analyst, Cisco Industrial Networking Specialist Certification, Electronic Security Networking Technician, Certified Network Computer Technician, Network Technology Associate, Certified Wireless Network Administrator, Certified Network Defender, GIAC Assessing and Auditing Wireless Networks, Certified Network Systems Technician, Certified Wireless Specialist, CompTIA Network+

Possible U.S. Salary Ranges[109]: $41,000-$78,000+

Similar U.S. Industry Job Titles[110]: Network Operations Specialist, Network Management Administration Specialist, Network Operations Center Engineer, Information Systems Security Specialist, Computer Specialist, Special Agent, Cyber Operations Specialist Principal, Information Technology Specialist (Network Services), Telecommunications Specialist, Security Specialist, Intelligence Specialist (Operations Support), Network Security Specialist, Senior Network Engineering Specialist, IT Specialist (Network Administrator)

---

[108] https://www.careeronestop.org/
[109] https://www.payscale.com/research/US/Job=Network_
Operations_Specialist/Salary
[110] https://www.indeed.com/

Summary

As you can see in this IT role, it is very technology-driven and detail-oriented. You will be analyzing and sifting through all types of activity and data on the networks in order to understand what is happening in your environment on a consistent basis, and will need to identify and protect the infrastructure and business assets from threats. Familiarize yourself with all the latest networking and scanning tools and operating system commands so you can stay on top of the new ways to defend and safeguard your organization.

Coaching Time[111]

Ask yourself these powerful coaching questions:

1. What are some unusual skills I have at my disposal?

2. What do I get complimented on the most?

3. What do I enjoy doing on a regular basis?

Quote of the Day

"A year from now you will wish you had started today."

~ Karen Lamb

---

[111] 549 Powerful Coaching Questions,
      www.thecoachingtoolscompany.com

34th NICE Framework IT Role

Job Title: Partner Integration Planner

Work to advance cooperation across organizational or national borders between cyber operations partners. Aid the integration of partner cyber teams by providing guidance, resources, and collaboration to develop best practices and facilitate organizational support for achieving objectives in integrated cyber actions.

IT Role Abilities:

- Ability to communicate complex information, concepts, or ideas in a confident and well-organized manner through verbal, written, and/or visual means.

- Ability to accurately and completely source all data used in intelligence, assessment, and/or planning products.

- Ability to adjust to and operate in a diverse, unpredictable, challenging, and fast-paced work environment.

- Ability to apply approved planning, development, and staffing processes.

- Ability to apply critical reading/thinking skills.

- Ability to collaborate effectively with others.

- Ability to coordinate cyber operations with other organization functions or support activities.

- Ability to develop or recommend planning solutions to problems and situations for which no precedent exists.

- Ability to effectively collaborate via virtual teams.

- Ability to exercise judgment when policies are not well-defined.

- Ability to function in a collaborative environment, seeking continuous consultation with other analysts and experts—both internal and external to the organization—to leverage analytical and technical expertise.

- Ability to identify external partners with common cyber operations interests.

- Ability to interpret and apply laws, regulations, policies, and guidance relevant to organization cyber objectives.

- Ability to interpret and understand complex and rapidly evolving concepts.

- Ability to participate as a member of planning teams, coordination groups, and task forces, as necessary.

- Ability to tailor technical and planning information to a customer's level of understanding.

Category: Collect and Operate

Specialty Area: Cyber Operational Planning

Suggested Education/Work Experience[112]: Bachelor's degree preferred; must have understanding and experience in higher headquarter's staff operations supporting a general officer.

---

[112] https //www.indeed.com

Funding Resources for Training (Scholarships may be available such as these): The HotelPlanner.com Graduate Technology Scholarship for Military Veterans, The Sweet Flow Digital Marketing Scholarship, AMS Centennial Fellowships, Technology Addiction Awareness Scholarship, INKAS Rising Star Scholarship, Zuckerman STEM Leadership Program, Hedy Lamarr Achievement Award for Emerging Leaders in Entertainment

Types of Industry Certifications[113]: Associate in Information Technology, Certified Global Meeting Planner, CompTIA IT Fundamentals, Certified IT Consultant, Information Technology Security, The Certified Information Privacy Professional/Information Technology, Advanced Law Enforcement Planner, Certified Planner of Professional Meetings, Certified Planner, Security Program Integration Professional Certification, Intelligence Planner Certification Program, Certified Information Technology Professional, Certified Law Enforcement Planner

Possible U.S. Salary Ranges[114]**:** $33,000-$178,000+

Similar U.S. Industry Job Titles[115]**:** Strategic Planner-Networks and Cloud IT Planning, Staff Program Planner-Critical Path Scheduling, Enterprise Planner, Program Planner, Site Integration Leader, Strategic Planner, Production Planner

---

[113] https://www.careeronestop.org/
[114] https://www.payscale.com/research/US/Employer=
Integration_Partners/Salary
[115] https://www.indeed.com/

Summary

As you can see in this IT role, the ability to collaborate, plan, organize, and manage virtual teams across borders will be necessary and expected in order to harmonize strategic roadmaps so the organization can meet its goals and objectives. Be prepared to break down complex information and materials and other important details to effectively communicate the requirements in plain language for all participants so others can act on these plans.

Coaching Time[116]

Ask yourself these powerful coaching questions:

1. How important is this to me REALLY?

2. What research could I do to help me find my first step?

3. Do I personally know someone who has reached this goal?

Quote of the Day

"We can't control what is happening, but we can keep choosing kindness."

~ Anonymous

---

[116] 549 Powerful Coaching Questions
www.thecoachingtoolscompany.com

National Initiative for Cybersecurity Education (NICE) Cybersecurity Workforce Framework

35th NICE Framework IT Role

Job Title: Privacy Officer/Privacy Compliance Manager

Develop and oversee privacy compliance program and privacy program staff, supporting privacy compliance, governance/policy, and incident response needs of privacy and security executives and their teams.

Category: Oversee and Govern

Specialty Area: Legal Advice and Advocacy

IT Role Abilities:

- Ability to develop clear directions and instructional materials.

- Ability to develop policy, plans, and strategy in compliance with laws, regulations, policies, and standards in support of organizational cyber activities.

- Ability to develop, update, and/or maintain standard operating procedures (SOPs).

- Ability to select the appropriate implant to achieve operational goals.

- Ability to tailor technical and planning information to a customer's level of understanding.

- Ability to monitor advancements in information privacy laws to ensure organizational adaptation and compliance.

- Ability to work across departments and business units to implement the organization's privacy principles and programs, and align privacy objectives with security objectives.

- Ablity to monitor advancements in information privacy technologies to ensure organizational adaptation and compliance.

- Ablity to determine whether a security incident violates a privacy principle or legal standard, requiring specific legal action.

- Ability to develop or procure curriculum that speaks to the topic at the appropriate level for the target.

- Ability to author a privacy disclosure statement based on current laws.

Suggested Education/Work Experience[117]: Bachelor's degree required; advanced degree preferred, and/or CHPC (Certified in Healthcare Privacy Compliance)

Funding Resources for Training (Scholarships may be available such as these): STC-PSC Scholarships, Jack M. Nagasaka Memorial Scholarship, AMS Graduate Fellowship in the History of Science, Material Handling Education Foundation Scholarships, DOE Office of Science Graduate Student Research (SCGSR) Program, Advanced Light Source Collaborative Postdoctoral Fellowship Program

Types of Industry Certifications[118]: Certified Information Privacy Manager, The Certified Information Privacy Professional, Certified HIPAA Professional, Certified Electronic Health Record Specialist, Certified FISMA Compliance Practitioner, Certified Medical Compliance Officer, Certified Information Privacy Technologist, Certified Professional Compliance Officer, Certified in

---

[117] https://www.indeed.com
[118] https://www.careeronestop.org/

Healthcare Privacy and Security, Associate in Regulation and Compliance, The Certified Information Privacy Professional/Information Technology

Possible U.S. Salary Ranges[119]: $58,000-$144,000+

Similar U.S. Industry Job Titles[120]: Privacy Officer, Compliance Manager, Privacy Manager, Privacy Analyst, Medical Practice Manager, Product Manager-Privacy and Compliance, Manager-Compliance, Info Sec Compliance Manager, Privacy Compliance Manager, Compliance Investigations Manager, Privacy Operations Specialist, Manager-HIPAA Privacy, Manager of Compliance and Privacy

Summary

In this IT role, there will need to be ongoing continuing education in privacy law, regulations, new policies, and technical privacy and security requirements so the required procedures can be implemented and communicated appropriately and diligently to your constituents in order to stay on top of compliance with all international, federal, state, and local laws and best practices related to your industry. Make every possible effort to track credible sources on a regular basis and stay in the know with your privacy communities and standard approving bodies of knowledge frameworks and other authorities.

---

[119] https://www.payscale.com/research/US/Job=Compliance
_%26_Privacy_Officer/Salary
[120] https://www.indeed.com/

Coaching Time[121]

Ask yourself these powerful coaching questions:

1. What do I stand for?

2. What would I stand up and fight for?

3. How do I think my thoughts could be getting in the way?

Quote of the Day

"Knowing yourself is the beginning of all wisdom."

~ *Aristotle*

---

[121] 549 Powerful Coaching Questions
www.thecoachingtoolscompany.com

National Initiative for Cybersecurity Education (NICE) Cybersecurity Workforce Framework

36th NICE Framework IT Role

Job Title: Product Support Manager

Manage the package of support functions required to field and maintain the readiness and operational capability of systems and components.

Category: Oversee and Govern

Specialty Area: Program/Project Management and Acquisition

IT Role Abilities:

- Ability to apply supply chain risk management standards.

- Ability to conduct and implement market research to understand government and industry capabilities and appropriate pricing.

- Ability to oversee the development and update of the life cycle cost estimate.

- Ability to evaluate/ensure the trustworthiness of the supplier and/or product.

- Ability to ensure security practices are followed throughout the acquisition process.

Suggested Education/Work Experience[122]**:** Minimum education required; must have at least 4-7 years of relevant Product Management, Product Owner, Business Analyst, and/or System Analyst experience; and suggested Agile software product development environment preferred.

Funding Resources for Training (Scholarships may be available such as these): Frederick A. Tarantino Memorial Scholarship Award, E.I. Dupont Graduate Fellowship, Vessa Notchev Fellowship (VNF), John R. Sevier Memorial Scholarship Award, David C. Lizarraga Graduate Fellowships, CyberCorps ®: Scholarship for Service, Michael Baker Corp. Scholarship for Diversity in Engineering

Types of Industry Certifications[123]**:** Certified Brand Manager, Product Safety Design Engineer, Agile Certified Product Manager, Certified Product Manager, Certified Technology Manager, Certified Senior Technology Manager, Certified Product Safety Manager, New Product Development Professional

Possible U.S. Salary Ranges[124]**:** $55,000-$117,000+

Similar U.S. Industry Job Titles[125]**:** Technology Product Manager, Product Manager, Product Launch Manager, Product Support Manager, Software Product Manager, Information Technology Manager, Technical Product Manager, Management, Lead Product Manager, Product Development Manager

---

[122] https://www.indeed.com
[123] https://www.careeronestop.org/
[124] https://www.payscale.com/research/US/Job=Product_
Support_Manager/Salary
[125] https://www.indeed.com/

Summary

As you can see in this IT role, there will be a need to understand the acquisition process and product life cycle methodology along with some cost benefit analysis work. Be prepared to oversee a budget or cost center and be ready to be challenged on your financial projections or any other line-item expenses to avoid cost overruns and to meet other business needs. Management and delegation skills will be key to the successful product launch.

Coaching Time[126]

Ask yourself these powerful coaching questions:

1. What are some of my unusual skills?

2. Where am I too hard on myself?

3. What is it I believe that keeps me from fully being myself?

Quote of the Day

"Bravery is in the action, so do it afraid."

~ Sakinah Tanzil

---

[126] 549 Powerful Coaching Questions:
       www.thecoachingtoolscompany.com

National Initiative for Cybersecurity Education (NICE) Cybersecurity Workforce Framework

37th NICE Framework IT Role

Job Title: Program Manager

Lead, coordinate, communicate, integrate, and be accountable for the overall success of the program, ensuring alignment with agency or enterprise priorities.

Category: Oversee and Govern

Specialty Area: Program/Project Management and Acquisition

IT Role Abilities:

- Ability to apply supply chain risk management standards.

- Ability to oversee development and update of the life cycle cost estimate.

- Ability to evaluate/ensure trustworthiness of the supplier and/or product.

- Ability to ensure security practices are followed throughout the acquisition process.

Suggested Education/Work Experience[127]*:* Degree in Computer Science or Engineering preferred; and 10-12 years of industry experience with at least 5+ years as technical project manager delivering advanced analytics solutions as an individual contributor.

---

[127] https://www.indeed.com

Funding Resources for Training (Scholarships may be available such as these): Internet Society Fellowships to the IETF, Kathi Bowles Scholarships for Women in Technology, National Security Technologies Engineering and Science Scholarships, National Science Foundation Graduate Research Fellowship Program, Rieser Fellowships, (ISC)2 Foundation Information Security Scholarships

Types of Industry Certifications[128]: Certified for Program and Project Managers-Entry Level, Certified for Program and Project Manager- Mid Level, Certified for Program and Project Manager-Senior Level, Certified Technology Manager, Professional Cloud Security Manager Certification, Certified Senior Technology Manager, Certified Information Security Manager, Master Project Manager, GIAC Certified Project Manager, Certified International Project Manager, Project Manager E-business, Certified Information System Security Professional

Possible U.S. Salary Ranges[129]: $98,000-$172,000+

Similar U.S. Industry Job Titles[130]: Technical Program Manager, Senior Program Manager, Program Manager, Senior Program Manager, Senior Manager- Program Manager, Global Infrastructure Program Manager, Manager-Program Management, Information Security Program Manager

---

[128] https://www.careeronestop.org/
[129] https://www.salary.com/research/salary/benchmark/program-manager-salary
[130] https://www.indeed.com/

Summary

This was an IT leadership role that I personally was assigned to design, create, and lead as part of a 52-member team. This role allowed me to see the entire strategic planning process across the entire $7.5 billion organization where I was privileged to coordinate the whole Information Security and Privacy Department projects and initiatives. There was a lot of procurement work, tactical planning, project management, and program management involved, and I obtained a great deal of knowledge, skills, and new abilities that I did not know I had, which was very exciting, scary, and stressful, all at the same time. I learned so many intricate, private, and sensitive details about the culture of the organization, its massive upcoming projects, its financial health, and its progressive history. It was a very fascinating and eye-opening experience that I will never forget.

Coaching Time[131]

Ask yourself these powerful coaching questions:

1.   Who do I admire?

2.   What specifically do I admire about them?

3.   If there were three rules that EVERYONE must follow, what would they be?

Quote of the Day

"If you want it, work for it."

~ *Anonymous*

---

[131]   549 Powerful Coaching Questions
www.thecoachingtoolscompany.com

National Initiative for Cybersecurity Education (NICE) Cybersecurity Workforce Framework

38th NICE Framework IT Role

Job Title: Research & Development Specialist

Conduct software and systems engineering and software systems research to develop new capabilities, ensuring cybersecurity is fully integrated. Conduct comprehensive technology research to evaluate potential vulnerabilities in cyberspace systems.

Category: Securely Provision

Specialty Area: Technology R&D

IT Role Abilities:

- Ability to identify systemic security issues based on the analysis of vulnerability and configuration data.

- Ability to prepare and present briefings.

- Ability to produce technical documentation.

- Ability to identify critical infrastructure systems with information communication technology that were designed without system security considerations.

Suggested Education/Work Experience[132]*:* Bachelor's degree from an accredited college or university, with major course of work in Computer Science, Information Systems, Health Informatics, or other related field of study preferred. Minimum of 2 years of experience working in complex environments, preferably including full time in an organization's Information Technology division or department. Equivalent combinations of education and

---

[132] https://www.indeed.com

experience may be substituted to meet the education and experience requirements of this position.

Funding Resources for Training (Scholarships may be available such as these): Dolphins E. Milligan Graduate Fellowships, Nellie Yeoh Whetten Award, RA Consulting Service/Maria Riley Scholarships, Lendon N. GlaxoSmithKline-NOBCChE Fellowships, Vessa Notchev Fellowship (VNF), Albert Einstein Distinguished Educator Fellowship (AEF), China and East Asia Google PHD Fellowships

Types of Industry Certifications[133]: Associate in Information Technology, CompTIA IT Fundamentals, Information Technology Security, Certified in the Governance of Enterprise Risk, Certified Security Specialist, Information Technology Security Fundamentals, Cloud Technology Associate Certification, CompTIA A+ Certification.

Possible U.S. Salary Ranges[134]: $37,000-$100,000+

Similar U.S. Industry Job Titles[135]: IT Specialist, Supervisory IT Specialist, Acquisition Program Specialist, Product Owner, Intelligence Research Specialist, Instructional Development Specialist

Summary

As the T role title suggests, there will be a lot of research and development and fact-finding opportunities involved, with an increased ability to prepare a report and present your findings in qualitative and/or quantitative forms for others to understand what research

---

[133] https://www.careeronestop.org/
[134] https://www.payscale.com/research/US/Job=Information_Technology_Specialist/Salary
[135] https://www.indeed.com/

materials, studies, and other artifacts are being presented so the person interpreting this information can ultimately act on this data and information. Be prepared to back up your findings with evidence such as case studies that are peer-reviewed or have come from credible sources; otherwise, some of the findings may not be valuable or credible enough to hold its value. The people who will review this information will need to have the confidence that what is being presented is accurate and well-researched, which is critical to the success of the product, project, or program.

Coaching Time[136]

Ask yourself these powerful coaching questions:

1. What is the very decision I have been avoiding?

2. If there is an outcome or result I am secretly looking for, what could it be?

3. So, what is wrong with that?

Quote of the Day

"If you can dream it, you can do it."

~ Walt Disney

---

[136] 549 Powerful Coaching Questions
www.thecoachingtoolscompany.com

National Initiative for Cybersecurity Education (NICE) Cybersecurity Workforce Framework

39th NICE Framework IT Role

Job Title: Secure Software Assessor

Analyze the security of new or existing computer applications, software, or specialized utility programs and provides actionable results.

Category: Securely Provision

Specialty Area: Software Development

IT Role Abilities:

- Ability to use and understand complex mathematical concepts (e.g., discrete math).

- Ability to apply cybersecurity and privacy principles to organizational requirements (relevant to confidentiality, integrity, availability, authentication, non-repudiation).

- Ability to identify critical infrastructure systems with information communication technology that were designed without system security considerations.

Suggested Education/Work Experience[137]:

- High School Diploma/GED + 10 years of experience

- Associate Degree + 8 years of experience

- Bachelor's degree + 6 years of experience

- Master's degree + 4 years of experience

- Ph.D. + 2 years of experience

---

[137] https://www.indeed.com

Funding Resources for Training (Scholarships may be available such as these): John R. Sevier Memorial Scholarship Award, Anna Valicek Award, Air Products and Chemicals Inc. Scholarships, Women in Defense HORIZONS Scholarship, SHPE Dissertation Scholarship, $5000 Nitro Scholarship, The Thurgood Marshall College Fund, IAEM Scholarship Program, "Advice To Your High School Self" Scholarships

Types of Industry Certifications[138]: GIAC Secure Software Programmer, Certified Secure Software Lifecycle Professional, Certified Application Security Engineer, Certified Manager of Software Testing, Certified Associate in Software Testing, Certified Software Tester, Certified Software Business Analyst, Software Engineering Master Certification, Certified Secure Computer User, Certified Software Development Professional

Possible U.S. Salary Ranges[139]: $48,000-$134,000+

Similar U.S. Industry Job Titles[140]: Information Security Applications Code Assessor, Cybersecurity/Info Assurance/Sec Assessor, Security Control Assessor, Advanced Security Assessor, Information Assurance Services/PCI, Director of Information Security and Compliance, Senior Manager of Information Security, Software Assurance Assessor, Cyber Security Specialists, Principal Cybersecurity Tester/ Assessor, Cybersecurity Risk Analyst/Security Controls Assessor

---

[138] https://www.careeronestop.org/
[139] https://www.payscale.com/research/US/Job=Security_Assessor/Salary
[140] https://www.indeed.com/

Summary

As you can see in this IT role, there will need to be a clear understanding of science and mathematics, even as simple as understanding how the operating system and applicctions work, so you will be capable of identifying and troubleshooting the root cause of the issues. Also, be particularly familiar with how to conduct a security assessment and how to use testing protocols and procedures to validate, diagnose, and find answers to the problems that need a resolution.

Coaching Time[141]

Ask yourself these powerful coaching questions:

1. Which decision would be the QUICKEST to complete?

2. Which decision is the CHEAPEST?

3. What is the EASIEST way forward for me now?

Quote of the Day

"Never give up. Great things take time."

~ Anonymous

---

[141] 549 Powerful Coaching Questions
       www.thecoachingtoolscompany.com\

40th NICE Framework IT Role

Job Title: Security Architect

Ensure that the stakeholder security requirements necessary to protect the organization's mission and business processes are adequately addressed in all aspects of enterprise architecture, including reference models, segment and solution architectures, and the resulting systems supporting those missions and business processes.

Category: Securely Provision

Specialty Area: Systems Architecture

IT Role Abilities:

- Ability to apply the methods, standards, and approaches for describing, analyzing, and documenting an organization's enterprise information technology (IT) architecture (e.g., Open Group Architecture Framework [TOGAF], Department of Defense Architecture Framework [DoDAF], Federal Enterprise Architecture Framework [FEAF]).

- Ability to communicate effectively when writing.

- Ability to conduct vulnerability scans and recognize vulnerabilities in security systems.

- Ability to apply an organization's goals and objectives to develop and maintain architecture.

- Ability to optimize systems to meet enterprise performance requirements.

- Ability to apply network security architecture concepts including topology, protocols, components, and principles (e.g., application of defense-in-depth).

- Ability to apply secure system design tools, methods, and techniques.

- Ability to apply system design tools. methods, and techniques, including automated systems analysis and design tools.

- Ability to design architectures and frameworks.

- Ability to apply cybersecurity and privacy principles to organizational requirements (relevant to confidentiality, integrity, availability, authentication, and non-repudiation).

- Ability to serve as the primary liaison between the enterprise architect and the systems security engineer and coordinate with system owners, common control providers, and system security officers on the allocation of security controls as system-specific, hybrid, or common controls.

- Ability, in close coordination with system security officers, to advise authorizing officials, chief information officers, senior information security officers, and the senior accountable official for risk management/risk executive (function) on a range of security-related issues (e.g. establishing system boundaries; assessing the severity of weaknesses and deficiencies in the system; plans of action and milestones; risk mitigation approaches; security alerts; and potential adverse effects of identified vulnerabilities).

- Ability to identify critical infrastructure systems with information communication technology that were designed without system security considerations.

- Ability to set up physical or logical sub-networks that separate an internal local area network (LAN) from other untrusted networks.

Suggested Education/Work Experience[142]***:*** 5+ years related work experience or equivalent combination of transferable experience and education; preferred experience in security technology design, development and/or monitoring.

Funding Resources for Training (Scholarships may be available such as these): AfterCollege STEM Inclusion Scholarship, The Edwards Annual College Scholarships, Imagine America College Scholarships for High School Students, Mobile Application Development Scholarship Program, The Don Riebhoff Memorial Scholarship, Kids and Community Scholarship Program, CareerFitter Online Scholarship, Sweet & Simple Scholarship, Watson-Brown Scholarship

Types of Industry Certifications[143]***:*** Certified Network Defense Architect, Certified Information System Security-Architect, Professional Cloud Solutions Architect Certification, GIAC Continuous Monitoring Certification, GIAC Information Security Fundamentals, GIAC Security Leadership Certification, GIAC Security Essentials Certification, Certified Cyber Security Professional-Associate/ Practitioner, Systems Security Certified Practitioner, GIAC Information Security Professional, Certified Cyber Security Professional-Foundation,

---

[142] https://www.indeed.com
[143] https://www.careeronestop.org/

Associate of International Information System Security Certification Consortium

Possible U.S. Salary Ranges[144]: $86,000-$163,000+

Similar U.S. Industry Job Titles[145]: IT Security Architect, IT Specialist, Security Consultant, IT Infrastructure Manager, Supervisory IT Specialist, Vice President of IT, Information Security Architect, Director of Information Security, IT Cybersecurity Specialist, IT Security Manager, Information Security Engineer, IT Infrastructure and Security Architect, IT Program Manager, IT Manager, IT Technology Leader

Summary

As you can see in this IT role, architecture frameworks, protocols, and design knowledge will be essential to know and understand so you will be able to build security requirements in and to develop a more resilient infrastructure. Risk and vulnerability management will be necessary skills to understand and communicate to the proper authorized officials.

---

[144] https://www.payscale.com/research/US/Job=
       Security_Architect%2C_IT/Salary
[145] https://www.indeed.com/

Coaching Time[146]

Ask yourself these powerful coaching questions:

1. If I secretly knew the way forward from here, what would it be?

2. How do I feel about that?

3. What is the difference that would make the difference?

Quote of the Day

"Don't rush the process, good things take time."

~ *Author Unknown*

---

[146] 549 Powerful Coaching Questions
www.thecoachingtoolscompany.com

National Initiative for Cybersecurity Education (NICE) Cybersecurity Workforce Framework

41st NICE Framework IT Role

Job Title: Security Control Assessor

Conduct independent comprehensive assessments of the management, operational, and technical security controls and control enhancements employed within or inherited by an information technology (IT) system to determine the overall effectiveness of the controls (as defined in NIST SP 800-37).

Category: Securely Provision

Specialty Area: Risk Management

IT Role Abilities:

- Ability to identify systemic security issues based on the analysis of vulnerability and configuration data.
- Ability to answer questions in a clear and concise manner.
- Ability to ask clarifying questions.
- Ability to communicate complex information, concepts, or ideas in a confident and well-organized manner through verbal, written, and/or visual means.
- Ability to communicate effectively when writing.
- Ability to conduct vulnerability scans and recognize vulnerabilities in security systems.
- Ability to facilitate small-group discussions.
- Ability to prepare and present briefings.
- Ability to produce technical documentation.
- Ability to design valid and reliable assessments.
- Ability to analyze test data.

- Ability to collect, verify, and validate test data.

- Ability to dissect a problem and examine the interrelationships between data that may appear unrelated.

- Ability to identify basic common coding flaws at a high level.

- Ability to translate data and test results into evaluative conclusions.

- Ability to ensure security practices are followed throughout the acquisition process.

- Ability to apply collaborative skills and strategies.

- Ability to apply critical reading/thinking skills.

- Ability to effectively collaborate via virtual teams.

- Ability to evaluate information for reliability, validity, and relevance.

- Ability to evaluate, analyze, and synthesize large quantities of data (which may be fragmented and contradictory) into high-quality, fused-targeting/intelligence products.

- Ability to exercise judgment when policies are not well-defined.

- Ability to expand network access by conducting target analysis and collection to identify targets of interest.

- Ability to focus research efforts to meet the customer's decision-making needs.

- Ability to function effectively in a dynamic, fast-paced environment.

- Ability to function in a collaborative environment, seeking continuous consultation with other analysts and experts—both internal and external to the organization—to leverage analytical and technical expertise.

- Abiity to identify external partners with common cyber operations interests.

- Abiity to identify intelligence gaps.

- Abiity to identify/describe target vulnerability.

- Ability to identify/describe techniques/methods for conducting technical exploitation of the target.

- Ability to interpret and apply laws, regulations, polcies, and guidance relevant to organization cyber objectives.

- Abiity to interpret and translate customer requirements into operational action.

- Abiity to interpret and understand complex and rapidly-evolving concepts.

- Abiity to participate as a member of planning teams, coordination groups, and task forces, as necessary.

- Ability to recognize and mitigate cognitive biases wh ch may affect analysis.

- Ablity to think critically.

- Ablity to understand objectives and effects.

- Ablity to utilize multiple intelligence sources across all intelligence disciplines.

- Ablity to work across departments and business units to implement the organization's privacy principles and programs, and align privacy objectives with security objectives.

- Ability to monitor advancements in information privacy technologies to ensure organizational adaptation and compliance.

- Ability to develop or procure curriculum that speaks to the topic at the appropriate level for the target.

- Ability to work across departments and business units to implement the organization's privacy principles and programs, and align privacy objectives with security objectives.

- Ability to prioritize and allocate cybersecurity resources correctly and efficiently.

- Ability to relate strategy, business, and technology in the context of organizational dynamics.

- Ability to understand technology, management, and leadership issues related to organization processes and problem solving.

- Ability to understand the basic concepts and issues related to cyber and its organizational impact.

- Ability to apply cybersecurity and privacy principles to organizational requirements (relevant to confidentiality, integrity, availability, authentication, non-repudiation).

- Ability to identify critical infrastructure systems with information communication technology that were designed without system security considerations.

Suggested Education/Work Experience[147]:

- Bachelor of Science or Associate of Science degree in Computer Science/Engineering, Cyber Security, Information Systems Management, or other engineering discipline.

- 5+ years' experience in the field or related area.

---

[147] https://www.indeed.com

- Knowledge and experience identifying, assessing, and documenting compliance against applicable DoD security controls (technical, management, operational) regulations.

Funding Resources for Training (Scholarships may be available such as these): Giuliano Mazzetti Scholarship, Decommissioning and Environmental Science Division Graduate, Disabled Veterans Scholarship, Annual iSeeCars Future Entrepreneurs Scholarship, Rich Abjian Leadership Scholarship, Tsutako Curo Scholarship, The Angie Dipietro Women in Business Scholarships

Types of Industry Certifications[148]: GIAC Defensible Security Architecture, GIAC Critical Controls Certification, Global Industrial Cyber Security Professional, CompTIA Security +, GIAC Certified ISO-27000 Specialist, CSX Cybersecurity Practitioner, Certified Information Systems Auditor, GIAC Information Security Fundamentals, Certified in Risk and Information Systems Control, GIAC Security Leadership Certification, GIAC Security Essentials Certification, Certified Cyber Security Professional-Associate/Practitioner

Possible U.S. Salary Ranges[149]: $67,000-$96,000+

Similar U.S. Industry Job Titles[150]: Security Control Assessor-Senior, IT Security Analyst, Security Assessor, Information Technology Specialist, Cyber Security Controls Assessor, IT Specialist, Cybersecurity-Information Assurance Assessor, Security Control Assessors Representative, Information

---

[148]   https://www.careeronestop.org/
[149]   https://www.payscale.com/research/US/Job=Security_
        Control_Assessor/Salary
[150]   https://www.indeed.com/

System Security Officer, Specialist-Information System Security, Cybersecurity Third-Party Assurance Officer

Summary

As you can see in this IT role, you will need to understand the management, operational, and technical aspects of each infrastructure piece of the puzzle and be able to fully comprehend the role information technology plays in the overall strategy of the leadership team, its people, and processes of the overall system.

Coaching Time[151]

Ask yourself these powerful coaching questions:

1. If I were FULLY living my life, what is the first change I would start to make?

2. If I dare say it aloud, what would I make happen in my career or life right now?

3. What is my dream for this lifetime?

Quote of the Day

"There is no one giant step that does it; it's a lot of little steps."

~ Peter A. Cohen

---

[151] 549 Powerful Coaching Questions
www.thecoachingtoolscompany.com

National Initiative for Cybersecurity Education (NICE) Cybersecurity Workforce Framework

42nd NICE Framework IT Role

Job Title: Software Developer

Develop, create, maintain, and write/code new (or modify existing) computer applications, software, or specialized utility programs.

Category: Securely Provision

Specialty Area: Software Development

IT Role Abilities:

- Ability to tailor code analysis for application-specific concerns.

- Ability to use and understand complex mathematical concepts (e.g., discrete math).

- Ability to develop secure software according to secure software deployment methodologies, tools, and practices.

- Ability to apply cybersecurity and privacy principles to organizational requirements (relevant to confidentiality, integrity, availability, authentication, and non-repudiation).

- Ability to identify critical infrastructure systems with information communication technology that were designed without system security considerations.

Suggested Education/Work Experience[152]***:*** Bachelor of Science in Computer Science or Computer Engineering, with a focus on general programming, software design, software debugging, and proper documentation.

Funding Resources for Training (Scholarships may be available such as these): KnowBe4, INFOSEC, Exabeam Cybersecurity Scholarship Program, Morphisec Women in Cybersecurity Scholarship, Web Design Scholarship, Abe Voron Award, The Connor Group Kids & Community Partners Scholarship, McAllister Fellowship, Work Ethic Scholarship, Jungle Scholar, Affirm Scholarship Program

Types of Industry Certifications[153]: Certified Software Quality Analyst, Certified Manager of Software Testing, Certified Manager of Software Quality, Certified Associate in Software Testing, Certified Associate in Software Quality, Certified Software Tester, Certified Software Business Analyst, Software Engineering Master Certification, Certified Software Quality Engineer, Professional Software Engineer Process Master Certification, Certified Software Development Professional, Professional Cloud Developer Certification, Professional Software Developer Certification, Software Development Fundamentals, Associate Software Development Certification

Possible U.S. Salary Ranges[154]***:*** $50,000-$104,000+

Similar U.S. Industry Job Titles[155]***:*** Software Developer, Software Engineering Manager, Senior Software Engineer, Senior Software Developer, Software Engineer-Associate, Information Technology Specialist, IT Software

---

[152]   https://www.indeed.com
[153]   https://www.careeronestop.org/
[154]   https://www.payscale.com/research/US/Job=Software_
         Developer/Salary
[155]   https://www.indeed.com/

Engineer, Software Engineer, Entry Level Software Developer, Junior Software Developer

Summary

As you can see in this IT role, it will be particularly important to understand different programming languages and discrete math concepts to develop sound software programs. It will also be extremely beneficial to understand secure coding so that you build security in on the front end and not as an afterthought.

Coaching Time[156]

Ask yourself these powerful coaching questions:

1.   What is going to be my contribution to this world?

2.   What parts of myself am I dying to let out?

3.   Who would I like to be going forward?

Quote of the Day

"The beautiful thing about learning is that no one can take it away from you."

~ B. B. King

---

[156] 549 Powerful Coaching Questions
        www.thecoachingtoolscompany.com

National Initiative for Cybersecurity Education (NICE) Cybersecurity Workforce Framework

43rd NICE Framework IT Role

Job Title: System Administrator

Responsible for setting up and maintaining a system or specific components of a system (e.g., installing, configuring, and updating hardware and software; establishing and managing user accounts; overseeing or conducting backup and recovery tasks; implementing operational and technical security controls; and adhering to organizational security policies and procedures).

Category: Operate and Maintain

Specialty Area: Systems Administration

IT Role Abilities:

- Ability to conduct a comprehensive assessment of the management, and operational and technical security controls and control enhancements employed within or inherited by a system to determine the effectiveness of the controls (i.e., the extent to which the security controls are implemented correctly, operating as intended, and producing the desired outcome with respect to meeting the security requirements for the system).

- Ability to ensure that functional and security requirements are appropriately addressed in a contract, and that the contractor meets the functional and security requirements as stated in the contract.

Suggested Education/Work Experience[157]:

Experience:

- System administration: 1 year (Required)

Education:

- Associate Degree (Preferred)

Funding Resources for Training (Scholarships may be available such as these): NANOG Scholarship Program, EAPSI Fellowships, Two Year/Community Broadcast Education Association Scholarship, Paul Evan Peters Fellowship, Ben C. Francis Risk Management Education Fund, DOE Computational Science Graduate Fellowship (DOE CSGF), Dvora Brodie Scholarships, Google Lime Scholarship

Types of Industry Certifications[158]: Oracle Solaris 11 System Administration, IBM Certified Advanced System Administrator, IBM Certified System Administrator, Cisco and NetApp FlexPod Implementation and Administration Specialist, Linux Foundation Certified Engineer, NetApp Certified Storage Associate, Information System Analyst, Web Server Administration Certification, SAP Certified Technology Associate

Possible U.S. Salary Ranges[159]: $45,000-$88,000+

Similar U.S. Industry Job Titles[160]: IT Systems Administrator-Junior, System Administrator, IT System Administrator, UNIX Administrator, Systems Administrator, AWS System Administrator, Junior Systems Administrator, IT Administrator, Information Technology Systems Administrator, Associate Systems Administrator

---

[157] https://www.indeed.com
[158] https://www.careeronestop.org/
[159] https://www.payscale.com/research/US/Job=Systems_
    Administrator/Salary
[160] https://www.indeed.com/

Summary

As you can see in this IT role, there is minimal experience required to obtain a job position, but I do suggest you try to aim for a 4-year college degree, at least one certification, and some work experience so your chances of landing lucrative pay is more probable; then, you will be more sought after by many employers.

Coaching Time[161]

Ask yourself these powerful coaching questions:

1. Imagine it is a year from now and you have accomplished your goal. What steps have you taken to achieve it?

2. What are the crazy and wacky things you can do to meet your goal?

3. Suppose you have all the information you need. What would be the next step?

Quote of the Day

"Big things often have small beginnings."

~ Lawrence of Arabia

---

[161] 549 Powerful Coaching Questions
www.thecoachingtoolscompany.com

National Initiative for Cybersecurity Education (NICE) Cybersecurity Workforce Framework

44th NICE Framework IT Role

Job Title: System Testing and Evaluation Specialist

Plan, prepare, and execute tests of systems to evaluate results against specifications and requirements as well as analyze/report test results.

Category: Securely Provision

Specialty Area: Test and Evaluation

IT Role Abilities:

- Ability to analyze test data.

- Ability to collect, verify, and validate test data.

- Ability to translate data and test results into evaluative conclusions.

- Ability to apply cybersecurity and privacy principles to organizational requirements (relevant to confidentiality, integrity, availability, authentication, non-repudiation).

Suggested Education/Work Experience[162]: This type of a position may require a Bachelor's degree in a STEM field of study and 6 years' experience in conducting testing and evaluations, such as on military operations.

Funding Resources for Training (Scholarships may be available such as these): ScienceSoft Scholarship, AFCEA Cyber Studies and Intelligence Scholarships, CIA Undergraduate Scholarships, CFR National Intelligence Fellowships, Proven Data Recovery Technology

---

162 https://www.indeed.com

Scholarships, International Affairs Fellowships in Nuclear Security (IAF-NS)

Types of Industry Certifications[163]:   Certified Reliability Engineer, Certified Quality Engineer, ISA Certified Control System Technician, Cisco Telepresence Solutions Specialist, Certified Systems Engineering Professional, Certified in Risk and Information Systems Control, Certified Wireless Specialist

Possible U.S. Salary Ranges[164]: $28,000-$77,000+

Similar U.S. Industry Job Titles[165]:   Test and Evaluation Specialist, Industrial Specialist, Operations Test and Evaluation Specialist, Program Evaluation Specialist, Program System Specialist, Support Service Specialist, Standardization and Evaluation Specialist

Summary

As you can see in this IT role, testing and evaluation of data will be the main priority of the job, so that information systems and industry standards can be verified against it and attested to for production. It will be helpful to have a strong testing procedure or step-by-step checklist or protocol that is verifiable and accurately followed.

---

163   https://www.careeronestop.org/
164   https://www.payscale.com/research/US/Job=Evaluation_ Specialist/Salary
165   https://www.indeed.com/

Coaching Time[166]

Ask yourself these powerful coaching questions:

1. If I could see myself through the eyes of someone who genuinely loves and respects me, what new things would I see? (Make a list.)

2. Where could I be more forgiving and understanding of myself?

3. What is wrong with me just the way I am?

Quote of the Day

"Hold fast to dreams, for if dreams die, life is a broken winged bird that cannot fly."

~ Langston Hughes

---

[166] *549 Powerful Coaching Questions*
www.thecoachingtoolscompany.com

National Initiative for Cybersecurity Education (NICE) Cybersecurity Workforce Framework

45th NICE Framework IT Role

Job Title: Systems Developer

Design, develop, test, and evaluate information systems throughout the systems development life cycle.

Category: Securely Provision

Specialty Area: Systems Development

IT Role Abilities:

- Ability to apply cybersecurity and privacy principles to organizational requirements (relevant to confidentiality, integrity, availability, authentication, non-repudiation).

- Ability to identify critical infrastructure systems with information communication technology that were designed without system security considerations.

Suggested Education/Work Experience[167]: Requires a Bachelor's or foreign equivalent degree in Computer Science, Electrical Engineering, or a related field.

Funding Resources for Training (Scholarships may be available such as these): McMurray STEM-Scholarship Opportunity, NVIDIA Graduate Fellowships, Vectorworks Design Scholarship, IISE Presidents Scholarship, IISE Council of Fellows Undergraduate Scholarship, Career Awards at the Scientific Interface (CASI)

Types of Industry Certifications[168]: Professional Cloud Developer Certification, Certified Information Systems Security Professional-Engineering, Certified Information Systems Security Professional-Architecture, Microsoft

---

[167] https://www.indeed.com
[168] https://www.careeronestop.org/

Certified: Azure Developer Associate, AWS Certified Developer-Associate, IBM Certified Associate Developer, Microsoft Certified Solutions Developer, SAP Certified Development Associate, Software Engineering Master Certification, Red Hat Certified Architect

Possible U.S. Salary Ranges[169]: $49,000-$94,000+

Similar U.S. Industry Job Titles[170]: Software Developer-Systems Software, Jr. Software Developer, Software Developer Associate, Dot Net Developer, Java/J2EE Developer, C++ Software Developer, Salesforce Admin/Developer, Senior Full Stack Developer, Web Developer

Summary

As you can see in this IT role, there will need to be an understanding of design and development of the information system, and you will need to understand privacy and security requirements so these are built into the architecture. Be familiar with different computer programming languages and industry standards.

Coaching Time[171]

Ask yourself these powerful coaching questions:

1.   What do I avoid?

2.   What would I stand up and fight for?

3.   What would I risk my reputation over?

Quote of the Day

"If you learn self-control, you can master anything."

~ Author Unknown

---

[169]   https://www.payscale.com/research/US/Job=Systems_ Developer/Salary
[170]   https://www.indeed.com/
[171]   549 Powerful Coaching Questions
       www.thecoachingtoolscompany.com

National Initiative for Cybersecurity Education (NICE) Cybersecurity Workforce Framework

46th NICE Framework IT Role

Job Title: Systems Requirements Planner

Consult with customers to evaluate functional requirements and translate functional requirements into technical solutions.

Category: Securely Provision

Specialty Area: Systems Requirements Planning

IT Role Abilities:

- Ability to interpret and translate customer requirements into operational capabilities.

- Ability to apply cybersecurity and privacy principles to organizational requirements (relevant to confidentiality, integrity, availability, authentication, non-repudiation).

- Ability to identify critical infrastructure systems with information communication technology that were designed without system security considerations.

Suggested Education/Work Experience[172]: Bachelor of Arts or Bachelor of Science and 3+ years of experience with Information Operations (IO).

Funding Resources for Training (Scholarships may be available such as these): Getty Foundation Library Research Grants, Lawrence Fellowship, The Ludo Frevel Crystallography Scholarship, The Affirmative Action Student Scholarship Mini-Grant Travel Awards, Latinos in

---

[172] https://www.indeed.com

Technology Scholarship, Public Health Informatics Fellowship Program (PHIFP), American Association of Family and Consumer Sciences Undergraduate, EHA Exploratory Travel and Data Grants

Types of Industry Certifications[173]: Wireless Systems Installer Engineer, Systems Diagnostics and Troubleshooting, Systems Analysis, Certification Authorization Professional, Software Business Analysis, Fiber Optics Technician

Possible U.S. Salary Ranges[174]: $71,613-$93,585+

Similar U.S. Industry Job Titles[175]: Information Operations Planner, Cyber Exercise Planner, Operations Demand/Supply Planner, Continuity of Operations Planner, Planner/Analyst, Cyber Analyst, Network Planner

Summary

As you can see in this IT role, you will need to be a good listener and be able to document business requirements and turn them into the proper functional requirements so the software developer can build those requirements and business details into the information system the business needs. All forms of communication skills will be necessary for this role.

---

[173] https://www.careeronestop.org/

[174] https://www.salary.com/research/salary/listing/information-operations-planner-salary#:~:text=How%20much%20does%20an%20Information,falls%20between%20%2471%2C613%20and%20%2493%2C585."
https://www.salary.com/research/salary/listing/information-operations-planner-salary#:~:text=How%20much%20does%20an%20Information,falls%20between%20%2471%2C613%20and%20%2493%2C585.

[175] https://www.indeed.com/

Coaching Time[176]

Ask yourself these powerful coaching questions:

1. Who drains me?

2. Who can I hang out with, so achieving my goals becomes natural?

3. How can I teach people to treat me the way I want to be treated?

Quote of the Day

"Knowing that you don't know is a form of intelligence."

~ Socrates

---

[176] 549 Powerful Coaching Questions
www.thecoachingtoolscompany.com

National Initiative for Cybersecurity Education (NICE) Cybersecurity Workforce Framework

47th NICE Framework IT Role

Job Title: Systems Security Analyst

Responsible for the analysis and development of the integration, testing, operations, and maintenance of systems security.

Category: Operate and Maintain

Specialty Area: Systems Analysis

IT Role Abilities:

- Ability to conduct vulnerability scans and recognize vulnerabilities in security systems.

- Ability to apply cybersecurity and privacy principles to organizational requirements (relevant to confidentiality, integrity, availability, authentication, non-repudiation).

Suggested Education/Work Experience[177]:

- Minimum of 2 years of relevant experience in functional responsibility.

- Minimum Education: Bachelor Degree.

Funding Resources for Training (Scholarships may be available such as these): AWN Mathematics Travel Grants, Finnegan Diversity Scholarship, Mathematics Mentoring Travel Grants, Work Ethic Scholarship, The Steve Duckett Local Conservation Scholarships, Presidential Scholarship, AISES Oracle Academy

---

[177] https://www.indeed.com

Scholarship, American Association of Blacks in Energy Scholarship

Types of Industry Certifications[178]: GIAC Information Security Fundamentals, Associate of International Information Systems Security Certification Consortium, Certification in Risk and Information System Security, Certified Cloud Security Professional, GIAC Information Security Professional, System Security Certified Practitioner, EC-Council Certified Security Analyst, Certified Information Security Manager, GIAC Security Essentials Certification, CompTIA Advanced Security Practitioner

Possible U.S. Salary Ranges[179]: $48,000-$99,000+

Similar U.S. Industry Job Titles[180]: Security Analyst, Applications Analyst, Global Security Investigative Analyst, Business Systems Analyst, Systems Analyst, Junior Acquisition Analyst, IT Security Analyst, Information Security Analyst, Enterprise Security Analyst, Associate Operations Analyst, Global Security Operations Center Analyst, System Security Analyst

Summary

In this IT role, there will be a lot of analysis of systems for development and integration and testing of systems and their vulnerabilities, so the knowledge of the latest tools and the software lifecycle will be necessary for success in this position. Be sure to have good processes and a step-by-step checklist in place for easier testing procedures to follow and more consistency.

---

[178] https://www.careeronestop.org/
[179] https://www.payscale.com/research/US/Job=Security_
       Analyst/Salary
[180] https://www.indeed.com/

Coaching Time[181]

Ask yourself these powerful coaching questions:

1. What do I know already about what I was created to do?

2. How would a good friend describe what I am like? Which of those traits seem to stand out to others?

3. What is my most outstanding personality trait?

Quote of the Day

"Character is the part of your personality that people tend to admire, respect, and cherish."

~ The Power of Character Strengths

---

[181] Coaching Questions: A Coach's Guide to Powerful Asking Skills by Tony Stoltzfus

48th NICE Framework IT Role

Job Title: Target Developer

Perform target system analysis, build and/or maintain electronic target folders to include inputs from environment preparation, and/or internal or external intelligence sources. Coordinate with partner target activities and intelligence organizations and present candidate targets for vetting and validation.

Category: Analyze

Specialty Area: Targets

IT Role Abilities:

- Ability to communicate complex information, concepts, or ideas in a confident and well-organized manner through verbal, written, and/or visual means.

- Ability to accurately and completely source all data used in intelligence, assessment and/or planning products.

- Ability to clearly articulate intelligence requirements into well-formulated research questions and requests for information.

- Ability to develop or recommend analytic approaches or solutions to problems and situations for which information is incomplete or for which no precedent exists.

- Ability to evaluate, analyze, and synthesize large quantities of data (which may be fragmented and contradictory) into high-quality, fused-targeting/intelligence products.

- Ability to exercise judgment when policies are not well-defined.

- Ability to focus research efforts to meet the customer's decision-making needs.

- Ability to function effectively in a dynamic, fast-paced environment.

- Ability to function in a collaborative environment, seeking continuous consultation with other analysts and experts—both internal and external to the organization—to leverage analytical and technical expertise.

- Ability to identify intelligence gaps.

- Ability to recognize and mitigate cognitive biases which may affect analysis.

- Ability to recognize and mitigate deception in reporting and analysis.

- Ability to think critically.

- Ability to utilize multiple intelligence sources across all intelligence disciplines.

Suggested Education/Work Experience[182]:

- Education: Bachelor's (Required)

- Experience: Software Development, 7 years (Preferred)

Funding Resources for Training (Scholarships may be available such as these): National Federation of the Blind Scholarship Program, Jungle Scholar, Ralph W. Shrader Diversity Scholarship, CitizenshipTest.org Engineering and Science Scholarship, Applied Social Issues Internship Program, VIP Women in Technology Scholarship, Sam L.

---

[182] https://www.indeed.com

Booke Sr. Scholarship, Rentec Direct's Tech Mastery Scholarship

***Types of Industry Certifications*[183]:**   Certified Network Systems Technician, Certified Associate in Software Quality, Software Engineering Master Certification, Certified Manager of Software Testing, Certified Software Business Analyst, Certified Software Tester, Certified Software Quality Analyst, Certified Associate in Software Testing, Certified Manager of Software Quality, Certified Software Development Professional, Professional Cloud Developer Certification, Professional Software Engineering Process Master Certification

***Possible U.S. Salary Ranges*[184]:** $49,000-$94,000+

***Similar U.S. Industry Job Titles*[185]:** Application/Software Developer, Troubled Asset Specialist, Software Tester, Software Developer, Application Software Developer, Software Developer/Systems Software, Software Systems Developer, Application Developer, IS-Systems Developer, Information Technology Specialist

Summary

In this IT role, there will be a lot of intelligence gathering and analysis of information systems for threats and weaknesses. You will need to be a good communicator and have critical thinking and great consulting skills in order advocate for your results.

---

[183] https://www.careeronestop.org/
[184] https://www.payscale.com/research/US/Job=Systems_Developer/Salary
[185] https://www.indeed.com/

Coaching Time[186]

Ask yourself these powerful coaching questions:

1. What was my original vision when I first read this book?

2. What would I like to be doing five years from now?

3. What part of that could I begin doing now?

Quote of the Day

"Stay focused on your goals, your peace, and your happiness. Don't waste your time on anything that doesn't contribute to your growth."

~ *Inspirational Quotes* *www.pinterest.com*

---

[186] Stolkzfus, Tony (2008), Coaching Questions: A Coach's Guide to Powerful Asking Skills

Job Title: Target Network Analyst

Conduct advanced analysis of collection and open-source data to ensure target continuity, and to profile targets and their activities; develop techniques to gain more target information. Determine how targets communicate, move, operate, and live based on knowledge of target technologies, digital networks, and the applications on them.

Category: Analyze

Specialty Area: Targets

IT Role Abilities:

- Ability to communicate complex information, concepts, or ideas in a confident and well-organized manner through verbal, written, and/or visual means.

- Ability to accurately and completely source all data used in intelligence, assessment, and/or planning products.

- Ability to clearly articulate intelligence requirements into well-formulated research questions and requests for information.

- Ability to develop or recommend analytic approaches or solutions to problems and situations for which information is incomplete or for which no precedent exists.

- Ability to evaluate, analyze, and synthesize large quantities of data (which may be fragmented and contradictory) into high-quality, fused-targeting/intelligence products.

- Ablity to exercise judgment when policies are not well-defined.

- Ablity to focus research efforts to meet the customer's decision-making needs.

- Ablity to function effectively in a dynamic, fast-paced environment.

- Ablity to function in a collaborative environment, seeking continuous consultation with other analysts and experts—both internal and external to the organization—to leverage analytical and technical expertise.

- Ability to identify intelligence gaps.

- Ability to recognize and mitigate cognitive biases which may affect analysis.

- Ability to recognize and mitigate deception in reporting and analysis.

- Ability to think critically.

- Ability to utilize multiple intelligence sources across all intelligence disciplines.

Suggested Education/Work Experience[187]:   Minimum qualifications for this position require a Computer Science/Computer Engineering degree OR a degree that demonstrates a concentration of Computer Science coursework. For example, degrees in Computer Networking, Information Science, Information Systems, Information Technology, Information Security, Information Assurance, Cyber Security, and Digital Forensics MAY be considered for this position IF your coursework/transcripts

---

[187]   https://www.indeed.com

demonstrate a concentration of Computer Science coursework. Foundational Computer Science coursework includes the following courses: Computer Architecture, Programming Languages, Data Structures, and Algorithms.

Funding Resources for Training (Scholarships may be available such as these): AHETEMS Professional Scholarships, AISES Intel Growing the Legacy Scholarship Program, AVS MEMS and NEMS Technical Group Best Paper Award, SDE Fellowship, SHPE Dissertation Scholarship, United Engineering Foundation Grants

Types of Industry Certifications[188]: GIAC Certified Perimeter Protection Analyst, GIAC Continuous Monitoring Certification, Certified Wireless Network Administrator, Certified Network Defender, GIAC Certified Firewall Analyst, GIAC Certified Intrusion Analyst, Wireshark Certified Network Analyst, Certified Network Systems Technician, Network Technology Associate, Certified Network Computer Technician, CompTIA Network+, GIAC Network Forensics Analyst

Possible U.S. Salary Ranges[189]: $49,000-$132,000+

Similar U.S. Industry Job Titles[190]: Target Digital Network Analyst, Digital Network Exploitation Analyst, Systems Administrator, Digital Network Intelligence Analyst, Senior Analyst-Data and Analysis, Programmer Analyst, Data Analyst, Digital Forensics Analyst

---

[188] https://www.careeronestop.org/
[189] https://www.glassdoor.com/Salaries/target-digital-network-analyst-salary-SRCH_KO0,30.htm
[190] https://www.indeed.com/

Summary

As you can see in this IT role, there will be vast amounts of data that will need to be analyzed and turned into actionable data, and the ability to be unbiased and to use sound judgment in information gathering will be critical. Communication skills will be paramount in the sharing of this data.

Coaching Time[191]

Ask yourself these powerful coaching questions:

1. What is exciting about this new opportunity?

2. What makes this worth pursuing?

3. What does being faced with this decision now say about where I am in life?

Quote of the Day

"You've got what it takes, but it will take everything you've got."

~ Author Unknown

---

[191] Stoltzfus, Tony (2008), Coaching Questions: A Coach's Guide to Powerful Asking Skills

National Initiative for Cybersecurity Education (NICE) Cybersecurity Workforce Framework

50th NICE Framework IT Role

Job Title: Technical Support Specialist

Provide technical support to customers who need assistance utilizing client-level hardware and software in accordance with established or approved organizational process components (i.e., Master Incident Management Plan, when applicable).

Category: Operate and Maintain

Specialty Area: Customer Service and Technical Support

IT Role Abilities:

- Ability to accurately define incidents, problems, and events in the trouble ticketing system.
- Ability to develop, update, and/or maintain standard operating procedures (SOPs).
- Ability to design capabilities to find solutions to less common and more complex system problems.

Suggested Education/Work Experience[192]:

- 1 year of experience with desktop operating systems, including Windows and Mac OS X
- 1 year of application support experience
- 1 year of direct customer service experience
- 1 year of support experience, troubleshooting hardware and software problems

---

[192] https://www.indeed.com

- 1 year of professional experience with current Windows OS, Apple OS and hardware, Microsoft Office suite as well as Enterprise email and communication tools

- Proficiency in the Microsoft Office suite

- Knowledge of basic computer hardware

Funding Resources for Training (Scholarships may be available such as these): Ralph W. Shrader Diversity Scholarship, Nortel Scholarship, E. I. DuPont Graduate Fellowship, Dolphus E. Milligan Graduate Fellowships, ESA Foundation Scholarship, Eastman Kodak Dr. Theophilus Sorrell Fellowships, NOBCChE Procter and Gamble Fellowships

Types of Industry Certifications[193]: Computer Technical Support Certification, Network Technical Support Certification, CompTIA A+, CompTIA Network+, Certified Technical Professional, Technical Help Desk (Microsoft)

Possible U.S. Salary Range[194]s: $36,000-$80,000+

Similar U.S. Industry Job Titles[195]: Technical Support Specialist, Associate Technical Support Specialist, Technical Installation and Support Specialist, Senior User Support Specialist, Technical Support/Product Specialist, Senior Technical Support Specialist

Summary

In this IT role, customer service skills will be exceptionally important to have because you may be working with all levels of the organization and will need a lot of oral and written communication expertise to manage the

---

[193] https://www.careeronestop.org/
[194] https://www.payscale.com/research/US/Job=Technical_Support_Specialist/Salary
[195] https://www.indeed.com/

situation. Problem solving and troubleshooting root cause analysis knowledge will be a key function of this job.

Coaching Time[196]

Ask yourself these powerful coaching questions:

1. What is the dream or the compelling future that calls me right now?

2. Where do I see things going?

3. What is the best possible outcome?

Quote of the Day

"What you do today can improve all your tomorrows."

~ Ralph Marston

---

[196] Stoltzfus, Tony (2008): Coaching Questions, A Coach's Guide to Powerful Asking Skills

**National Initiative for Cybersecurity Education (NICE)
Cybersecurity Workforce Framework**

51st NICE Framework IT Role

Job Title: Threat/Warning Analyst

Develop cyber indicators to maintain awareness of the status of the highly dynamic operating environment. Collect, process, analyze, and disseminate cyber threat/warning assessments.

Category: Analyze

Specialty Area: Threat Analysis

IT Role Abilities:

- Ability to communicate complex information, concepts, or ideas in a confident and well-organized manner through verbal, written, and/or visual means.

- Ability to accurately and completely source all data used in intelligence, assessment, and/or planning products.

- Ability to clearly articulate intelligence requirements into well-formulated research questions and data tracking variables for inquiry tracking purposes.

- Ability to develop or recommend analytic approaches or solutions to problems and situations for which information is incomplete or for which no precedent exists.

- Ability to effectively collaborate via virtual teams.

- Ability to evaluate information for reliability, validity, and relevance.

- Ability to evaluate, analyze, and synthesize large quantities of data (which may be fragmented and contradictory) into high-quality, fused-targeting/intelligence products.

- Ability to focus research efforts to meet the customer's decision-making needs.

- Ability to function effectively in a dynamic, fast-paced environment.

- Ability to function in a collaborative environment, seeking continuous consultation with other analysts and experts—both internal and external to the organization—to leverage analytical and technical expertise.

- Ability to identify intelligence gaps.

- Ability to recognize and mitigate cognitive biases which may affect analysis.

- Ability to recognize and mitigate deception in reporting and analysis.

- Ability to think critically.

- Ability to think like threat actors.

- Ability to utilize multiple intelligence sources across all intelligence disciplines.

Suggested Education/Work Experience[197]:

- High school diploma and a minimum of 0-5 years of relevant experience, OR college degree and 0-2 years relevant work experience.

- Ability to obtain a top-secret clearance.

- Basic network understanding.

---

[197]   https://www.indeed.com

- Basic understanding of security best practices.

- Good verbal, interpersonal, and written communication skills.

- Good analytical, problem-solving, and decision-making capabilities.

Funding Resources for Training (Scholarships may be available such as these): Margaret Dowell-Gravatt M.D. Scholarship, NANOG Scholarship Program, NIJ Visiting Fellows Program, DEPS Graduate Scholarship, International Code Council Scholarship, ASH Foundation New Century Scholars Research Grant

Types of Industry Certifications[198]: GIAC Cyber Threat Intelligence, Cyber Threat Intelligence Analyst, GIAC Defending Advanced Threats, Certified Cyber Security Professional-Foundation, Certified Cyber Resilience Professional, Associate Cyber Resilience Professional

Possible U.S. Salary Ranges[199]: $100,066-$128,533+

Similar U.S. Industry Job Titles[200]: Cyber Threat Analyst, Space and Cyber Intelligence Analyst, Computer Network Analyst, Cyber Security Analyst, Associate Cyber Intelligence Analyst, Security Services Specialist, Cyber Analyst, NIS Threat Intelligence Analyst, Threat Analyst, Cyber Operations Analyst, Cyber Defense Analyst

Summary

As you can see in this IT role, intelligence gathering, analytical decision-making skills, and result-driven data and facts will be paramount in successfully performing in this position. There will be multiple sources of data points that will need to be made into visual examples and stories

---

[198] https://www.careeronestop.org/
[199] https://www.salary.com/research/salary/listing/cyber-threat-analyst-salary
[200] https://www.indeed.com/

in order to explain in detail the types of threats and the necessary actions the individual or organization will need to take to stay protected and up and running.

Coaching Time[201]

Ask yourself these powerful coaching questions:

1. Can you create a job description that is a perfect fit for who you are?

2. What would make your ideal job significant or fulfilling to you?

3. Imagine you are working in an organization that is a perfect fit for you. What would be the organizational culture and values?

Quote of the Day

"Your career, your job, is very important, but who you are as a person, your values and beliefs, are most important."
~ *Kenneth Chenault*

---

[201] Stoltzfus, Tony (2008), Coaching Questions: A Coach's Guide to Powerful Asking Skills

National Initiative for Cybersecurity Education (NICE) Cybersecurity Workforce Framework

52nd NICE Framework IT Role

Job Title: Vulnerability Assessment Analyst

Perform assessments of systems and networks within the network environment or enclave, and identify where those systems/networks deviate from acceptable configurations, enclave policy, or local policy. Measure effectiveness of defense-in-depth architecture against known vulnerabilities.

Category: Protect and Defend

Specialty Area: Vulnerability Assessment and Management

IT Role Abilities:

- Ability to identify systemic security issues based on the analysis of vulnerability and configuration data.

- Ability to apply programming language structures (e.g., source code review) and logic.

- Ability to share meaningful insights about the context of an organization's threat environment that improve its risk management posture.

- Ability to apply cybersecurity and privacy principles to organizational requirements (relevant to confidentiality, integrity, availability, authentication, non-repudiation).

Suggested Education/Work Experience[202]:

- 5+ years of experience in Cybersecurity

- Demonstrate expertise and track record in Web, Mobile, Network, and System Application Penetration testing (Web, Mobile, API/Web Services)

- Experience using Tools for Firewall Evasion, Abuses to IPSec VPN, Border Gateway Protocol, GRE Tunneling

- Expertise in penetration testing methodology

- Experience in developing exploits and tooling from vulnerabilities both pre-exploitation and post-exploitation

Funding Resources for Training (Scholarships may be available such as these): OAS Scholarship for Professional Development-The ABC of Innovative Grants-Pilot and Research Tools Grants, Herbert Roback Scholarship, ISDS Graduate Student Scholarship, Public Service Internship-Research and Program Evaluation, Woodrow Wilson-Rockefeller Brothers Fund Fellowships for Aspiring, Finnegan Diversity Scholarship

Types of Industry Certifications[203]: Certified in Control Self-Assessment, GIAC Assessing and Auditing Wireless Networks, Information Security Analyst, Certified Web Analyst, CompTIA Cybersecurity Analyst, GIAC Certified Intrusion Analyst, Certified Software Quality Analyst, GIAC Certified Forensic Analyst, Criminal Intelligence Certified Analyst, Wireshark Certified Network Analyst, GIAC Certified Detection Analyst

Possible U.S. Salary Ranges[204]: $64,789-$95,592+

---

202 https://www.indeed.com
203 https://www.careeronestop.org/
204 https://www.indeed.com/career/information-security-analyst/salaries

Similar U.S. Industry Job Titles[205]*:* Vulnerability Assessment Analyst, Strategic IT Analyst, Defense Assessment Analyst/Penetration Tester, Information Security Analyst, Cybersecurity Analyst, Threat Analyst, Web Application Vulnerability Analyst, IT Professional, Cyber Network Intelligence Analyst, Vulnerability Management Analyst, Cyber Software Analyst, SOC Analyst, Vulnerability Infrastructure Assessment Analyst

Summary

In this IT role, there will be a need to understand programming languages and configuration standards. Understanding security flaws and cyber threats will be key. Being familiar with firewalls and other security infrastructure tools will be necessary in protecting the overall information system.

Coaching Time[206]

Ask yourself these powerful coaching questions:

1. If I could spend my life working to change one thing in the world that would make a real difference for others, what would that one thing be?

2. If I think back over the last ninety days, who have I gone out of my way to help in a big way or small? What drew me to each of these people?

3. What world-changing dream makes my heart beat faster?

Quote of the Day

"A diamond is a piece of charcoal that handled stress exceptionally well."

~ Unknown

---

[205] https://www.indeed.com/
[206] Stoltzfus, Tony (2008): Coaching Questions, A Coach's Guide to Powerful Asking Skills

www.ingramcontent.com/pod-product-compliance
Lightning Source LLC
Chambersburg PA
CBHW071331210326
41597CB00015B/1407